The Mindful Our Father

Thomas G. Casey SJ

Published by Messenger Publications, 2022.

ISBN: 9781788125796

Cover image © Shutterstock
Typeset in Adobe Caslon Pro, Adobe Garamond Pro & Sabon LT Pro
Printed by Hussar Books

Messenger Publications,
37 Leeson Place, Dublin D02 E5V0
www.messenger.ie

DEDICATION

To Joshua, Thomas, and David

Much more is accomplished by a single word of the Our Father said, now and then, from our heart, than by the whole prayer repeated many times in haste and without attention.
St Teresa of Ávila

The Our Father contains all possible petitions; we cannot conceive of any prayer not already contained in it. It is to prayer what Christ is to humanity. It is impossible to say it once through, giving the fullest possible attention to each word, without a change, infinitesimal perhaps but real, taking place in the soul.
Simone Weil

Sometimes when I am in such a state of spiritual dryness that not a single good thought occurs to me, I say very slowly the Our Father, or the Hail Mary, and these prayers suffice to take me out of myself, and wonderfully refresh me.
St Thérèse of Lisieux

Table of Contents

Introduction

Lord, teach us to pray ... (Lk 11:1)

Praying the Our Father as Though for the First Time
An elderly monk reached a high level of holiness. His fellow monks wanted to know how this came about, but his humility made him hesitant to speak about himself. One day he let down his guard with a close friend. 'It was through reciting the Our Father', he explained. His friend was taken aback, 'You mean you arrived at such heights through that simple prayer?' The old monk nodded. He added, 'I was more surprised than anyone. You know, for years I had forced myself to try all sorts of unusual prayers. And after all that time, everything was so utterly straightforward. In fact, when I finally discovered how uncomplicated the path was, I felt like a real fool.'

'Why did you feel so foolish?' asked his friend. 'Because', replied the holy monk, 'I was like someone who purchases a high security key to open a bank vault, only to discover that the treasure is in fact lying in full view in front of me.'

The Lord's Prayer is so familiar that we don't realise what a treasure it truly is. We try out new kinds of prayers, but don't appreciate the wonder of this prayer that is right in front of us.

The Lord's Prayer is a simple prayer that goes back to Jesus. But even though it has been around for such a long time, we no longer know how to pray it as it deserves to be prayed. We grow up saying this prayer in a hurried way, we continue to recite it in a rush, and we risk dying without ever waking up to its richness.

In this book I'm not offering a new formula for prayer. I'm not presenting a new blueprint for how to communicate with God. Instead, I'm going back to what is most familiar in the hope that we will recognise it for the first time. It is all too easy to neglect or overlook the important things. We are like the hapless prefect of police in Edgar Allan Poe's short story 'The Purloined Letter'. The puzzled police chief is mystified by the theft of a letter, which is now being used to blackmail the person from whom it was stolen. The chief knows for certain that the thief is a government minister. Despite searching the minister's house with a fine comb from top to bottom, his men have come up with nothing. The prefect of police turns for help to Dupin, a detective with an eccentric nature – and a gifted mind. Unlike the policeman, Dupin gives credit to the thieving minister for being intelligent, and therefore assumes that the politician is too clever to do what the policeman expects – conceal the letter in an elaborate hiding place. Dupin figures correctly that the minister will do precisely the opposite. Where do you hide something that you don't want people to discover? Dupin guesses correctly that the minister has not hidden the letter in an obscure place, but in the most conspicuous place possible.

The riches of the Our Father are right in front of us – they are contained in the prayer itself. My hope is that this book will rekindle your desire to unearth the marvellous treasures concealed in this familiar prayer. The Our Father is like a house with a deep basement, extending several floors into the earth, and a high roof, reaching all the way up to heaven. Most of us have only visited the ground floor, so we think that there isn't that much to the Our Father. In reality, we have only uncovered a fraction of its riches. That's because too often we have reduced the Lord's Prayer to a series of standardised formulae. This book aims to give you a better view of the deep foundation and upper floors of this powerful prayer. Within this apparently mundane prayer, there are astonishing riches. You can access these riches quite simply: by giving yourself time to ponder its wonder. Once you get a sense of the dimensions of this iconic prayer that Jesus taught, you will find yourself led to pray it with renewed fervour and devotion.

To find the best way to pray the Our Father, you do not need to travel to a holy place or special shrine. You already have all you need – here and now. It's just that you have only noticed a tiny part of it. This is the moment to look at the Lord's Prayer afresh and see it with new eyes.

These pages are written to re-connect you with the fullness that is hidden in this seminal prayer. In *Middlemarch*, her wonderfully wise and compassionate novel, George Eliot (whose real name was Mary Ann Evans) wrote: 'If we had a keen vision and feeling of all ordinary human life, it would be like hearing the grass grow and the squirrel's heartbeat, and we should die of that roar which lies on the other side of silence. As it is, the quickest of us walk about well-wadded with stupidity.' We need to develop a 'keen vision and feeling' for the Our Father, this apparently ordinary prayer. As George Eliot remarks, it's all too easy to 'walk about well-wadded with stupidity'. It is less easy to notice what is truly important.

Love Is at the Heart of the Lord's Prayer

What, then, is the really important truth to notice about the Our Father? That our loving desire for God is at the heart of this prayer, just as our love for God is at the heart of all true prayer.

A lot of people have not woken up to the fact that love is the core of prayer. But we won't know how to pray well until we learn this secret. Instead, we will be tempted to believe that the more we speak, the more God will listen to us. The truth is that as long as we only utter words, we have not yet begun to pray. As King Claudius rightly observes in Shakespeare's *Hamlet*: 'My words fly up, my thoughts remain below. Words without thoughts never to heaven go.' God has so much he wants to give us. The greater our love, the more we can receive. It is not our words that open up the riches of God's goodness: it is the longing of our hearts. If we reach out to God with the whole energy of our being, we shall certainly find God. In his treatise *On the Lord's Prayer*, St Cyprian writes, 'God listens, not to the voice, but to the heart, and since he reads our thoughts, he does not need to have his attention called by clamour.'

We only start to pray when we start to love, because love is the litmus test of all prayer. Have I loved? If so, then I have also prayed. Do I love? If so, then I am really praying. Am I growing in love? If so, my prayer is deepening as well.

Jesus taught us that prayer is love by teaching us the Our Father, because every line of this prayer has something to teach us about love. The first loving aspect to this prayer is that we begin by loving God enough to place ourselves before him as 'Our Father'. We begin by contemplating his tenderness and greatness. We ask that he may be loved and that his eternal plan may be realised. In other words, we start this prayer by focusing on God and not on ourselves. As a rule, when we pray, we instinctively give first priority to our own needs: we tell God what we want. We don't pause long enough to consider his desires. The Lord's Prayer teaches us to put God and his plans in first place.

We begin the Lord's Prayer by addressing God as Father, as someone who has a close and even intimate relationship with us. We immediately go on to say that this Father of ours is in heaven, and therefore transcendent. Heaven is where true life is, because this is where love reigns. Once we've established who God is (our Father) and where he is (in heaven), the seven petitions of the Lord's Prayer begin, and each of them has something important to say about love.

After turning to the Father in heaven, the first three petitions are divine in their direction – thy name be hallowed, thy kingdom come and thy will be done. We ask for God's name to be hallowed, and we achieve this by making his love transparent before everyone. We pray for God's kingdom to come: in other words, for God's reign of love to become real in our hearts and in our world. We ask for God's will to be done on earth, and this request is fulfilled when we truly love both God and our neighbour.

The final four petitions are for ourselves – give us, forgive us, lead us and deliver us. We ask for bread and sustenance, not just for ourselves as individuals, but for everyone. Although this petition expresses great trust in God's providential care, it is a limited request, limited to a single day: 'give us *this day* our daily bread'. We don't ask to win the lottery; we don't ask for enough wealth to keep us comfortable and secure for the rest of our lives.

We go on to ask God to forgive us for our unwillingness to be generous in loving, and we also plead for the grace to forgive as he does. Jesus teaches us here that the love we receive from God is directly linked to the love we extend toward our neighbours.

We ask for help when we're tempted and for encouragement when we feel like closing the shutters because we've been wounded and hurt too often. In those difficult moments, we look for the strength to trust and love as Jesus did. It's striking that we don't ask to escape suffering, but to be delivered from evil. Suffering can be an evil, but suffering and evil are not always the same thing. Certainly, we're asking to be delivered from suffering to the extent that it is an evil. But at the same time, if suffering works for our good, we're at least open to accepting it. What is most important is to be freed from anything and everything that undermines our relationship with God – whatever breaks our bond with God is the real evil.

As well as teaching us the Lord's Prayer, Jesus himself helps us identify the pivotal petition in this prayer. During his agony in the Garden of Gethsemane, on the eve of his Crucifixion, Jesus says to the Father – 'not my will, but thine be done'. Surrendering our own will to God is the central and defining struggle that love asks of us. 'Thy will be done on earth as it is in heaven' is pivotal because it is crucially important, but it is also a pivot or turning point. Up until this petition the prayer has gone 'God-ward' (Our Father, thy name, thy kingdom, thy will), and after it the prayer goes 'we-ward' (give us, forgive us…).

The Lord's Prayer Should Be in Every Prayer

In the early fifth century, a widow named Anicia Faltonia Proba contacted St Augustine, asking him to teach her how to pray. He wrote back a lengthy letter and made a truly striking observation – any prayer we say should be inspired by the spirit of the Lord's Prayer, and if it's not, then it's not genuine prayer. Augustine isn't saying that we must use the precise words of the Lord's Prayer in our own prayers, but he is saying that we need to stay in harmony with its basic thrust. We are free to use the words we want, but our prayers should go in the same direction as the Our Father. The authenticity of our prayers depends on how closely they harmonise with the attitudes and sentiments expressed in the Lord's Prayer.

Augustine takes scriptural prayers as the prime example of prayers that are in tune with the Our Father. He says that if we go through all the prayers contained in the Bible, we shall find that each one is contained in the Lord's Prayer, and every biblical prayer finds its fulfilment in the Our Father.

Augustine also gives an example of the kind of prayer that is *not* authentic: if I pray to obtain power, wealth or fame, simply to benefit from these, and not to use them to help others live in a more Christian way, that kind of prayer is not genuine because it does not fit in with any of the requests in the Lord's Prayer. We should be ashamed to ask God for such things. But if we find ourselves overwhelmed with these kinds of toxic desires, we can always ask God to free us from them by using these or similar words: 'deliver us from evil'.

According to Augustine, the Lord's Prayer teaches us the things we should desire and should seek in our lives. And it also shows us the order in which we should search for them: starting with God – Our Father – and then moving on to ourselves. The Lord's Prayer is a compendium of everything we could possibly ask God. It is the perfect résumé of the spiritual life.

Threefold Structure
Each chapter of this book focuses on a phrase from the Lord's Prayer. Every phrase is approached from several angles. With the addition of thought-provoking stories and stimulating prayers, the intention is to awaken a deeper understanding of the Lord's Prayer. There are three basic ingredients in each chapter: seeking the meaning of the particular phrase of the Our Father that we are exploring, letting relevant stories touch our hearts and getting into the habit of praying ourselves.

We seek the meaning of each phrase. We need to look for the meaning because the wisdom of the Lord's Prayer is not immediately obvious. There is a real need to reflect and meditate on each phrase, to 'chew' on the words as a cow would chew on the cud, to find the marrow of meaning, and so discover true nourishment. It is like digging for hidden treasure. In each chapter I approach the various parts of the Our Father from multiple perspectives, in order to facilitate a deepening level of engagement with its richness.

By going through the Lord's Prayer phrase by phrase, it is possible to taste something of the unique flavour of each line. As the Lord says to the prophet Ezekiel: 'Son of man, eat this scroll that I am giving you and fill your stomach with it' (Ezek 3:3). The prophet eats it and remarks that it tastes 'as sweet as honey in my mouth'. But beyond tasting and eating, there is another step: digestion. If you can digest the words, they will become part of you. Interestingly, when Ezekiel digests the scroll, it releases a bitter flavour in his stomach. This is not necessarily a bad sign, because according to ancient tradition, what is bitter also detoxifies the system and so purifies and heals. So even if you find some of the content of this prayer initially challenging, don't let that deter you: it could just be the threshold to deep healing.

We allow stories to touch our hearts. Why stories? There are so many good reasons. Stories shape and re-shape our lives. It is through stories that we make sense of ourselves and our world. Stories give a pattern to the chaos of life and bestow meaning on otherwise random events. Stories give new perspectives and help us see concretely how we can live wisely and well. Stories also connect us with people. They give us an inside view of how other people feel and think. This inside view shows us what we have in common with others and at times challenges our own ways of seeing things. Through stories we can receive the grace of becoming kinder and more compassionate human beings. Stories are universal in their reach. They 'speak', in the widest sense of the word. They open us up to a deep part of ourselves, a place where we are linked with other people and with our shared history. And crucially, stories make important points in easy-to-remember ways that intrigue us and capture our attention.

We start praying ourselves. There will be several short prayers scattered throughout our various chapters. Why these prayers? After all, isn't the Lord's Prayer itself more than enough? Well, yes and no. The Our Father is enough, because it is the fullness of all prayer; it's not enough, because everyone needs help to unearth its riches. The prayers that finish every section of each chapter are ultimately there to help you enter more deeply into the Our Father. These prayers are down-to-earth. They are real and relevant, flavoured with honesty and hope. Please God, they will help you on your journey.

In this introductory chapter, there won't be prayers at the end of each section. However, in partial compensation, there will be a long mindful prayer at the end of the introduction, and just before the first chapter begins. This lengthy prayer will relate to the petition 'thy will be done'. The will of God is the foundation of all things, their beginning and their end. It is the most profound and definitive reality, both on earth as it is in heaven.

A Practical Approach to the Our Father

Millions of Christians around the world recite the Lord's prayer, both individually and when they come together for worship. This prayer appears in both the Gospel of Matthew and the Gospel of Luke. In Chapter 6 of Matthew's Gospel, Jesus is sitting on the mountainside, speaking to his disciples and to the crowds who have gathered there. He warns them not to use empty phrases or to babble on when they pray, and offers instead as a model the Our Father. In the Gospel of Luke – sometimes called the 'gospel of prayer' because Jesus teaches a lot about prayer in this Gospel and is also depicted praying more frequently than in the other three Gospels combined – one of his disciples asks him, 'Lord, teach us to pray' (Lk 11:1). In response, Jesus immediately prays the Our Father.

I'll leave it to the scholars to explain why there are two (really similar) versions of the Our Father in the New Testament, the short version in Luke with five petitions, and the slightly longer version in Matthew, made up of seven petitions. I'll leave it to biblical experts to speculate on what these two versions tell us about the early Christian communities in which they were composed, and how the first Christians understood this prayer.

My focus is on how the Our Father can speak to us today and how it can enrich our lives. I take as my basis the Our Father as Christians ordinarily pray it. I will include the phrase – 'for the kingdom, the power and the glory are yours, now and for ever'. This phrase is used in the Reformed Churches and is also recited at the end of the Lord's Prayer during Mass in the Roman Catholic Church. Here is the version of the Our Father upon which I draw in this book, but of course please feel free to use the version that is most conducive to prayer:

Our Father, who art in heaven, hallowed be thy name.
Thy kingdom come.
Thy will be done on earth, as it is in heaven.
Give us this day our daily bread,
and forgive us our trespasses,
as we forgive those who trespass against us.
And lead us not into temptation, but deliver us from evil.
For the kingdom, the power and the glory are yours, now and for ever.

In the Gospel of Matthew, Jesus teaches the Our Father during his longest recorded sermon ever – the Sermon on the Mount. As well as being the longest sermon of Jesus, this is also the first sermon Jesus gives in Matthew's Gospel. It is three chapters long (chapters 5, 6 and 7 of Matthew's Gospel). It gets its name from the fact that Jesus goes up a mountain to deliver it. The Sermon on the Mount describes the key principles of Christian life. The Our Father occurs right in the middle of the Sermon of the Mount, as though to highlight its centrality and importance. Scholars agree that the Sermon on the Mount conveys the heart of Jesus' teaching. And at the heart of this heart of the teaching of Jesus we find the Our Father.

In the first four chapters of Matthew's Gospel, God is never referred to as Father. But once Jesus launches into the Sermon on the Mount, things change completely, for Jesus mentions the Father more often in the Sermon on the Mount than the Father is mentioned in the entire Hebrew Bible or Old Testament. Jesus, then, begins his public ministry in Matthew by emphasising the centrality of the Father and the importance of this prayer addressed to him.

From a Help to a Hindrance and Back Again
Jesus gave us the Our Father to help us pray. Yet this strong support has almost become a hindrance. Many of us know the Our Father

by heart. When we want to speak to God but aren't sure what to say, this is the familiar prayer we turn to. We recite it as if it were a formula. In doing so, we come close to the caricature of prayer Jesus warned us against, 'And when you pray, do not keep babbling like pagans, for they think they will be heard because of their many words' (Mt 6:7).

This book provides a means to move away from a rapid-fire recitation of the Our Father. It is an invitation to pray it in a relaxed way. In his introductory remarks at the beginning of *The Spiritual Exercises*, St Ignatius of Loyola (1491–1556) observes that 'it is not knowing much, but realizing and relishing things interiorly, that contents and satisfies the soul'. To realize and relish things interiorly means to ponder on them, to mull over them and to let them sink into our hearts. It means not rushing from one moment of prayer to the next, but staying in the present moment long enough to savour it. If we're in a hurry, we won't stop long enough to see, listen and relish. We'll become mere consumers of our experiences, dumping them almost as soon as we have had them.

The Lord's Prayer is a pearl of great price and only reveals its beauty to the one who approaches it with awe, recites it with respect and savours its sweetness. We need to move from 'head knowledge' of the Our Father to 'heart knowledge' of it. The heart is only a matter of inches away from the head, but sometimes it can take a lifetime to move from one to the other. Over the course of our lives, we need to learn to pray the Our Father in a *mindful* and *heartfelt* way.

Here are two examples of praying the Our Father in a mindful and heartfelt way. One example comes from Ignatius of Loyola, the other from a French-Jewish mystic.

Ignatius of Loyola and the Our Father
Many people don't associate St Ignatius of Loyola with the Lord's Prayer. It's not that they think he looked down on it in any way. Instead, they take it for granted that he never gave this prayer much attention in his writings. When St Ignatius and prayer come

to mind, people often think of his creative use of the senses and imagination to enter into the stories of Scripture, or else they think of the reflective prayer – the examen – that gratefully reviews the events of a particular day.

St Ignatius actually gives an important place to the Our Father. Toward the end of his *Spiritual Exercises*, he applies the wisdom of 'relishing things interiorly' to the Lord's Prayer. His guidelines can be found in a section of the book called 'Three Methods of Prayer'. The second and third methods are contemplative ways of praying, and it is while explaining these second and third methods that Ignatius brings up the Lord's Prayer.

In the second method of prayer, Ignatius recommends praying the Our Father a word at a time, staying with each word as long as it continues to echo inside. The person is to avoid the impulse to rush ahead. Ignatius expresses it this way: 'If in contemplating the Our Father one finds in one or two words rich matter for reflection and much relish and consolation, there should be no anxiety to go further, even though the whole hour is spent on what has been found' (*Spiritual Exercises*, 254).

The third method is simpler – and even deeper. Here, Ignatius suggests synchronising each word of the Our Father with the rhythm of our breathing. Breath prayer is an ancient Christian form of prayer that has been practised for millennia. It is especially associated with Christians belonging to the Greek and Russian Orthodox Churches. St Paul encouraged Christians to pray without ceasing, and breath prayer offers a practical means of achieving this goal. The more constant our breath prayer, the closer we get to praying without ceasing.

Ignatius recommends praying a single word of the Our Father in rhythm with each breath we take. We maintain this pattern as we go through the Lord's Prayer, word by word. Uniting prayer with breathing is a physical and intimate kind of prayer. It is bodily prayer because it demands concentration on our breathing, and so relieves us from thinking too much and from being too taken up with our thoughts. It is an intimate kind of prayer because our very lives depend on drawing breath.

Simone Weil on the Lord's Prayer

Simone Weil (1909–1943) was an eccentric and brilliant French mystic, philosopher, factory worker and trade union activist. Born into an affluent and non-practicing Jewish family in Paris in the early years of the twentieth century, Simone Weil was attracted by Catholicism. She chose not to be baptised, because she wanted to remain an outsider.

A couple of years before she died, Simone Weil decided to learn the Our Father by heart. Not in her mother tongue, but in the original Greek in which it is written in the Gospels. She enjoyed reciting it so much that one summer as she harvested vines, not only did she begin each day by saying the Our Father in Greek, but continued to say it over and over again as she worked in the vineyard. From that time onwards, she made it her practice each morning to recite the Our Father from start to end with pure attention. Whenever she became distracted, even if only for a second, she started from the beginning again, until she could recite the Our Father with pure attention the whole way through.

Simone Weil is careful to warn us not to confuse attention with grinding our teeth or furrowing our brows. She writes, 'most often attention is confused with a kind of muscular effort.' She emphasises that attention is not about aggressively going after something. Instead, attention is a kind of waiting. It is keeping ourselves open to what is in front of us. So, attention is not about straining ourselves or putting in lots of effort; in fact, it's not about ourselves at all. The truth is that if we are always thinking about ourselves, it will be impossible to keep ourselves open to what is before us. By inviting us to pay attention, Simone Weil is also challenging us to change our way of looking at reality, so that we give a more central place to God and others, rather than stubbornly planting ourselves at the centre of the universe.

She is inviting us to be receptive, open, patient, quiet and calm. And to drop, at least for a while, the meetings, plans and deadlines that consume so much of our time and energy. She is inviting us to empty ourselves of ourselves. In other words, to forget about our own personal concerns for long enough to be filled with the longing for something outside ourselves. She tells a simple Inuit story of a crow searching for light in the darkness. The crow's desire and attention are so strong that the world becomes filled with light. Although the crow itself does not have the power to produce light, the intensity of its desire and the purity of its attention combine to draw down the light.

Youcat, the Youth Catechism of the Catholic Church, quotes the following words from Simone Weil in its section on prayer: 'Prayer is nothing other than attention in its purest form'.

For Simone Weil, prayer isn't about having warm feelings; prayer is about being mindfully aware of God. She once remarked, 'attention is the highest and purest form of generosity'. Through focusing with kindness on someone, I am looking at them as they are, and not as I would like them to be. This is a tremendous kind of generosity, because by doing this I am in a sense giving them themselves.

Applying Simone Weil's insights on attention to the Our Father, we could say that this prayer gradually becomes transparent if we can approach it with a patient stillness, with a contemplative openness and with our hearts immersed in the prayer, rather than in ourselves. Our English verb 'to attend' is linked with the French verb *attendre*, 'to wait for', 'to expect'. True attention is a kind of waiting. It is a kind of waiting that is thoughtful, a kind of waiting during which we set aside our own plans and preconceptions in order to allow the truth to enter into us. We don't pray the Our Father for the purpose of becoming stronger or more powerful or more holy, but so that God's power may grow and our own power may decrease. As John the Baptist once put it: 'He must increase and I must decrease' (Jn 3:30)

Where and When to Pray

To promote the right frame of mind for praying the Lord's Prayer and indeed for praying any form of prayer, it helps to give thought to where and when we should pray. First, it is important to find the right *place* to pray. Just before Jesus teaches the Our Father in the Gospel of Matthew, he emphasises that we should not make a show of praying before others in the synagogues or on the street corners. Instead, he says, 'whenever you pray, go into your room and shut the door and pray to your Father who is in secret' (Mt 6:6). St Catherine of Siena, the fourteenth-century Italian mystic, calls this inner room a spiritual cell, a cell that we bring everywhere, a cell that is filled both with self-knowledge and a deep awareness of God's great love for us. Catherine says that if the cell is only of self-knowledge, we'll be tempted to despair; and if it is only a cell of God's goodness to us, we'll be tempted to become big-headed and conceited.

St Catherine of Siena's idea is wonderful, but it is advice that is more suited to those who have already made some progress in prayer. When you begin, it's not so easy to connect with this spiritual cell in your heart. It's easier to start by locating a specific physical place in which to pray. If you want to cultivate inner silence, it helps to find a place of outer silence. Although it is often impossible to find total silence, it helps if you can choose a space where you are not likely to be disturbed by others. It may be enough to sit in your favourite armchair, kneel by your bed, or gaze out the window toward the sky. But you may also find it helpful to 'tweak' the space somewhat in order to create a peaceful and pleasing atmosphere. For instance, you could use candles instead of electric lights, and add a splash of beauty by placing a vase of flowers or a bowl of fruit in the appropriate place. If your space is inviting, you will feel more invited to pray.

When is a good time to pray? In the Gospels, we learn that Jesus prayed in the morning and at night. He rose early in the morning to pray (Mk 1:35). Before choosing the apostles, he spent the whole night in prayer (Lk 6:12). But as well as praying at the opening of the day and during the night, Jesus was in communion with the Father throughout the day. In other words, although he chose certain moments for formal prayer, his prayer was in fact continuous. He was bathed in a continual awareness of the Father. He was totally in tune with the Father; so much so that the Father was always speaking through him. Jesus put it this way, 'I have not spoken on my own, but the Father who sent me has himself has given me a commandment about what to say and what to speak' (Jn 12:49).

It would be great if you could make it your ultimate goal to imitate Jesus and 'pray without ceasing' (1 Thess 5:17). You can start by imitating Jesus' rhythm of formal prayer and making sure to pray both morning and evening.

Morning prayer is a good thing to do because Jesus did it. His days were filled with healing, preaching, teaching and saving. But he began each day by spending time alone with the Father. Prayer gave him energy to do good. It also gave him the strength to persevere in the midst of trials and difficulties: as he said, 'the Son can do nothing on his own' (Jn 5:19). He encountered more than his share of setbacks and frustrations. By relaxing into the reality of the Father's love at the dawn of each day, he received the strength to face up to everything that was thrown at him in the course of his days, up to and including the final humiliations that came his way during his passion and crucifixion.

By greeting God first thing in the morning, you give him a concrete sign that he has first priority in your life. You speak with the Lord before you speak with people. You immerse yourself in God before you get absorbed in the events of the day. You listen to the good news before you lend your ear to any other kind of news. You honour God before you show your respect for anyone else. You nourish your spirit before you feed your body.

We have a telling phrase in the Irish language, '*Tosach maith, leath na hoibre*' – a good start is half the work. It is easy to see how effective this principle is if we reflect upon how buildings our constructed. The foundation is the most crucial part of a house; it supports the entire construction. Any defects in the foundation will only compound defects further up the house. Morning prayer is crucial because it supports the entire day. If you neglect to give a strong foundation to your day, you don't have a solid base on which to build.

The great advantage of praying before going to bed is the opportunity to hand over your problems to the Father. Each sleep is a little death, and before he died Jesus said to the Father, 'Into your hands I commend my spirit'. St Augustine says that God is closer to us than we are to ourselves. God is so close to you that he is more than willing to take care of your worries so that you can sleep peacefully.

Sometimes peaceful sleep isn't possible. There are nights when you wake up, look at the clock and realise it is the middle of the night. You try to go back to sleep, but you have become agitated by feelings and fears. Your mind has started running and simply refuses to stop. No matter how many times you turn over and toss in your bed, you cannot make yourself go back to sleep. This can be deflating. But you could also see it as a personal and loving invitation from God. In the Garden of Gethsemane, Jesus says to his disciples: 'Couldn't you keep watch with me? (Mt 26:40).

When you wake up in the middle of the night, it is easier for God to get through to you, because your normal defences are down. Prayer in the depth of the night may just be God's best hope of spending quality time with you, so instead of getting frustrated that you cannot sleep, look at this interruption of your slumber as a gift, even if it is not the kind of gift you really wanted. Night prayer isn't always full of warm feelings, but it is raw and honest, and you will be surprised how easily you can pour out your heart to God. Not only that, but God will enable you find light in the midst of the literal (and metaphorical) darkness. With the help of the final petitions of the Lord's Prayer (lead us not into temptation, but deliver us from evil), you may just find the worries of the night transformed into the audacity of blind trust in God.

Preparing to Pray – the Body Gives Voice to the Soul
The body and soul do not exist alongside each other in an external kind of way, as butter is spread on bread. The body and the soul are intertwined, like the dancer and the dance. In the words of the poet William Butler Yeats: 'how can we know the dancer from the dance?' As a rule, people don't say, 'my soul is praying'. Each of us says, 'I am praying'.

The intertwined nature of body and soul is reflected in prayer. When you pray, don't imagine that it is only an affair of the soul. Prayer needs to be expressed in bodily ways – through your words, expressions and gestures. Allow your body to play a part in your prayer. For instance, if you feel the urge to adore God, you may find yourself drawn to pray on your knees or even to extend prostrate on the ground. We are earthly creatures, and when the knees or the whole length of the body touches the earth, we are acknowledging our dependence on God.

The body affects the soul. A few words of the tongue can have a massive impact on the movement of the heart. Take these three words, 'I love you'. When we say these words to God, we give new oxygen to our desire for him, we nourish our relationship with him, and we strengthen our bond with him.

Use bodily gestures to express the hidden energy of your soul and to give new strength to this energy. Bodily gestures can include everything from kissing your Bible as a sign of grateful love to speaking to God in a gentle whisper that expresses reverence.

Preparing to Pray – the Threefold Gaze

When people are invited to meet a dignitary or someone important, they often prepare themselves by dressing more formally, by making a special effort to be there on time, and so on.

It's also important to prepare yourself to enter into God's presence. Here is a simple way to do this is – by a threefold gaze: first, looking at God, second, at yourself and third, at the world around you.

First comes God. Just as the Lord's Prayer begins with God, so should every prayer. As you place yourself in God's presence, gaze downwards in reverence before God's holiness, bowing down before his greatness with a physical gesture. St Paul tells us in his letter to the Philippians that a day will come when every knee shall bow and every tongue confess that Jesus Christ is Lord. But even during the lifetime of Jesus, many people bowed before him, especially when they came to him for healing. While he was still only an infant, the Magi came into his presence and fell down in worship before him. Your physical posture is important, because outward signs of respect nourish inner reverence.

Second, turn your gaze toward yourself, and recognising your own fragility in the face of God's fullness, say, 'Lord, have mercy on me a sinner'. Notice that this phrase expresses sinfulness in a relational context: it is a recognition of our shortcomings in the context of our relationship with God. Many people have issues with the judgemental overtones involved in admitting sinfulness, but we can all agree that however kind and loving we are, none of us is perfect, and there are moments when every relationship becomes strained. Calling yourself a sinner does not mean castigating yourself for being horrid or nasty but admitting that you're not perfect and that there are blockages in your relationship with God. As a result, you're always in need of God's mercy.

The parable of the Pharisee and the tax collector in Luke's Gospel contrasts two men who go up to pray in the Temple in Jerusalem. The Pharisee spends the time of prayer praising himself (he is not really relating to God, but to all intents and purposes engaged in a monologue). The tax collector 'would not even lift up his eyes to heaven but was beating his breast and saying, "God, be merciful to me, a sinner"' (Lk 18:13). The tax collector relates to God, all the while recognising how much he needs God's mercy. The right attitude before God is to recognise that even if you are an outstand-ingly good person, you're still in need of God's healing and forgive-ness. A genuine plea for mercy always wins God's heart, precisely because it is so refreshingly honest.

Third, turn your gaze to all the people of the world who need you in different ways, and say, 'Lord, please save my brothers and sisters'. In his first Letter to Timothy, St Paul tells us that we should pray for everyone – not just for those we know and who are close to us, but also for those we don't know and who are far away. Paul explains that praying for everyone's salvation pleases God, since he 'wants everyone to be saved' (1 Tim 2:4). Since this is what God wants, this should also be what we want. Jesus came for the sake of each and every person; so, by praying for the salvation of everyone, we are making this desire of Jesus our own.

For my part, I offer my prayer to God through Mary. Mary knows intuitively what is lacking in me when I turn to God. She is aware of my fears and my frettings, my frailties and my frayed edges. Not in order to point the finger at me, but to make new wine out of the lukewarm water I'm in danger of offering to God. During the wedding at Cana, Mary noticed they had run out of wine. She didn't mortify the host by telling the guests that the wine was gone. Instead, she quietly turned to Jesus and said, 'They have no wine' (Jn 2:3). Mary is only too ready to step in for us when we're lacking. She will take our side and plead on our behalf. By turning to Mary, our prayer arrives at Jesus faster and more effectively: Mary is the express route. And it becomes the special joy of Jesus to offer a prayer made through Mary as a sweet fragrance to the Father, setting his perfect seal upon it with his infinite merits.

Prayer

As we conclude our introduction, let's try an exercise in mindful prayer. Divine Reading, more often known by its Latin name *Lectio Divina*, is a mindful kind of prayer that finds its roots in the Bible. It was developed in a systematic way by St Benedict and the early monastic tradition. Divine Reading is a way of prayer that embraces several different ways of communicating with God: reading the Word of God, pondering its meaning, expressing our thoughts and feelings, active listening to the whispering of the heart, and resting in God's presence.

This mindful form of prayer begins with reading (*Lectio*) the passage of Scripture in an unhurried way in order to get a general sense of all of it. It then goes on to meditate (*Meditatio*) upon it. At this point, we invite the Holy Spirit to move in our heart, so that a particular word or phrase may touch us more deeply. We then allow this meditation to lead us to a heart-to-heart exchange or prayer (*Oratio*), where we share with God how this passage is affecting us right now. Finally, having gone through the previous steps, we are now ready to rest in God's presence: this is the stage of contemplation (*Contemplatio*). And as we emerge from this prayer, we can ask how to put into action what we have learned.

In our particular prayer exercise here, we'll engage with the scene of the Annunciation from Luke's Gospel (Lk 1: 26–38). This engaging scene provides a captivating portrait of a woman who effectively says: 'thy will be done'.

Lectio: **what the Word says in itself**

In chapter one of Luke's Gospel, two different births are announced: that of John the Baptist and that of Jesus. The birth of John the Baptist is announced to Zechariah in the political capital of Judaea – the city of Jerusalem, and in the spiritual heart of Judaism – the Temple. The birth of Jesus is announced to Mary in the intimacy of her own home. Each birth is announced by the angel Gabriel, the same angel who appeared to Daniel and made reference to the future Messiah, 'the Prince of princes' (Dan 8:25).

Mary does not live in the important city of Jerusalem, but instead in the obscure town of Nazareth in Galilee. Even the manner of Gabriel's entrance into her life is less dramatic than in the case of Zechariah: the latter saw the angel 'standing at the right side of the altar of incense'. In the case of Mary, we're not even sure if she actually sees Gabriel; all we are sure of is that Mary hears the voice of this angel whose name means 'strength of God'.

When Gabriel greets Mary, he does not use her name. Instead, he calls her 'full of grace'; in Greek these three English words form a single word: *kecharitomene*. This word, which never appears anywhere else in the Bible or in Greek literature, could be even better translated as: 'the one who has always been full of grace'. It's a unique word for a unique woman in whom grace has reached its full plenitude. In the Bible, God often gives a new name to designate a new mission, and this particular new 'name' indicates that Mary is the one who is favoured by God in a special way. She has been filled with grace in such a way that Gabriel adds: 'the Lord is with you', making clear that God's help is at her side, echoing the words that the (unnamed) angel of the Lord pronounced to the warrior Gideon in the Book of Judges (Judg 6:12).

Mary is perplexed by the angel's words, and wonders what kind of greeting this might be. Despite her puzzlement, Gabriel senses Mary's underlying faith. Whereas Gabriel reprimanded Zechariah for his lack of faith, Gabriel reassures Mary, and his words unfold the meaning of the new name he has given her – 'full of grace'. Gabriel explains that she 'has found favour with God', that her son 'will be great', 'the Son of the Most High', and 'his kingdom will have no end'.

An apparent contradiction still bothers Mary: how can she conceive a child while remaining a virgin? Zechariah, doubting the angel's words, asked for a sign. Mary, trusting the angel's words, and presumably guessing that the angel's announcement is to take effect in a matter of hours or days, respectfully asks how his words can be fulfilled, given the fact that she is a virgin. The angel explains that the body of Jesus will be created by God's express power – 'the power of the Most High will overshadow you'. Mary's response is one of total availability: 'Here I am, the servant of the Lord, let it be done unto me according to your word'.

Meditatio: what the Word says to me/us

Unlike Zechariah, most of us don't encounter angels in dramatic settings such as the Temple of Jerusalem. But like Mary, in various low-key ways, we experience 'annunciations' in the midst of our everyday lives: for instance, through the beauty of a sunset that brings us to the threshold of wonder, through the words of Scripture that awaken desires that were long submerged, or through a love that calls us beyond our limited horizons. In these different ways, an angel enters our lives with a divine message.

Oratio: what the Word leads me/us to say

How can we be alert and attentive enough to notice the moments when God speaks to us? One way is through learning to review the past in a spirit of prayerful thanksgiving: each evening we can look back on the day, asking for light to see those moments when the Lord has visited us.

Contemplatio: being transformed by the Word

Jesus wasn't born immediately after his conception; Mary carried him for nine months in her womb. In a similar way, the seeds of new life we identify through prayer take time to grow. We can help to nourish them by remembering to place ourselves peacefully in God's presence.

Actio: **putting the Word into practice**
Identify one seed planted in you by the Holy Spirit – an encouraging word from a friend, a phrase in Scripture, an act of kindness in a moment of distress that renewed your hope in the goodness of others … Finally, ask God to help you plant seeds this week so that new life may blossom in the hearts of those around you.

CHAPTER ONE

The Opening Words

*In me there is … only a murmur of living water that whispers
within, 'Come to the Father'.*
St Ignatius of Antioch, *Letter to the Romans*

The Dutch artist Rembrandt, one of the greatest painters of all
time, completed *The Return of the Prodigal Son* during the last
couple of years of his life – he died in 1669. A decade previously,
he had been declared bankrupt. Despite being out of money, out
of favour and widowed, Rembrandt produced this masterpiece. It
depicts the moment the prodigal son of the biblical parable returns
to his father's embrace. The father's left hand is steady and strong,
giving powerful reassurance to his son. His right hand appears
softer and more feminine, as though with this hand he is holding
his son with a motherly caress of mercy. The contrast between
these hands captures something of the mystery of the heavenly
Father. Neither man nor woman, since he is God, the Father nevertheless exemplifies – and infinitely surpasses – the best qualities
of each.

Our
The first word of the Lord's Prayer is 'our'. When we pray this
prayer, we address it to *our* Father. And this means that God can
only be Father for us to the degree that we are sisters and brothers
for each other. If we cut ourselves off from our brothers and sisters,
by this act of withdrawal we also stop being children of God.

   In Book Seven of Fyodor Dostoevsky's epic novel *The Brothers
Karamazov*, there is a powerful story which illustrates that Christians cannot truly experience God's fatherhood without committing themselves to their fellow human beings. It is told by the
character Grushenka.

Once upon a time a wicked woman died. The demons quickly caught hold of her and dragged her down into a lake of fire. Meanwhile her guardian angel desperately tried to recall any good deed that this woman had ever done in life. Suddenly he remembered something. 'Once', he said to God, 'she dug up an onion in her garden and gave it to a woman who was begging.' God replied to her guardian angel, 'Take that onion, hold it out to her in the lake so that she can grab hold of it and be pulled out. If you can manage to pull her out of the lake, you may bring her to Paradise. However, if the onion breaks on the way, she'll have to remain in the lake of fire.' Immediately the angel flew to the woman. He held out the onion. 'Just catch hold of it,' he cried, 'and I'll do the rest.' The angel pulled her out slowly and carefully. But some other sinners in the lake, noticing what was happening, grabbed hold of the woman so that they too could be drawn out of the lake of fire. The woman became indignant. She lashed out in anger and kicked them. 'I'm the one who is getting pulled out', she shouted, 'not you. This is my onion, not yours.' As soon as the woman spoke these words, the onion broke. She fell back down into the lake of fire and is still burning there today. As for her poor angel, he turned away and wept bitterly.

This parable has many layers, just like an onion, and it would take too much work (and too many tears!) to peel away each one of them. The parable shows for instance that even the smallest act of kindness can have momentous consequences. But for my purposes here, it demonstrates that if we limit God and salvation to ourselves as individuals, our lifeline – the onion in this story – will break sooner rather than later. The woman is not undone by the fact that she has hardly done anything good in her whole life. Instead, heaven closes in her face because of her fixation on salvation for herself alone, and by her unwillingness to entertain the notion that others could also be chosen.

Martin Buber, the Jewish philosopher and religious thinker, has a striking phrase: 'In the beginning is relation'. The fundamental reality of our interrelatedness is expressed by the word 'our' – I'm in a relationship with God, and I'm also in a relationship with my brothers and sisters around me.

The first word of the Lord's Prayer makes clear that it is never good to pray alone. Although you may be physically alone, you should never be spiritually isolated. Even if you're in solitary confinement, you need never be by yourself. Everyone – and all of creation – can be present in your prayer.

The Lord's Prayer does not begin with the individual, but with much more: the prayer is not the 'my Father', but the Our Father. This prayer is an invitation to stop putting the self and the ego at the centre of everything. It is a summons to go beyond even my family, my friends, my social group and my nation. The word 'our' does not mean that a particular group possesses the Father, as though he were only special for us and not for others. In the Lord's Prayer, this word 'our' is not a possessive pronoun, as though the Father were only the possession of a select few. Instead, it indicates a totally new way of relating to God. The Father is the Father of all: young and old, rich and poor, saints and sinners. And yet, even though a Father to all, God does not love everyone in an impersonal way, as a crowd or as an anonymous mass. God loves each one as though that person were the only person in the entire world.

Since this prayer is the *Our* Father, if you limit yourself to praying in your own voice, you will only make a weak sound. In order to strengthen your voice, you can make a threefold connection.

First, place yourself alongside all your fellow human beings, by uniting your voice to the voices of everyone across the face of the earth. The voices of the greatest Christians of our time can make your own voice stronger. For your part, you can strengthen the weak voices of those who rarely or never turn to God. To make up for them, you can love God even more fervently in compensation.

Second, place yourself alongside all of creation as you pray. In his encyclical *Laudato Si'* from 2015, Pope Francis called Catholics and people of good will to a profound ecological conversion. He is inviting us to live in harmony with creation rather than dominating it. We need to remind ourselves of the bonds that connect us to the rest of creation. 'As part of the universe, called into being by one Father, all of us are linked by unseen bonds and together form a kind of universal family' (*Laudato Si'*, 89). We need to reimagine our way of seeing ourselves: not as autonomous beings but as inter-dependent creatures. 'God wills the interdependence of creatures. The sun and the moon, the cedar and the little flower, the eagle and the sparrow: the spectacle of their countless diversities and inequalities tells us that no creature is self-sufficient. Creatures exist only in dependence on each other, to complete each other, in the service of each other' (*The Catechism of the Catholic Church*, 340).

The rain, the wind, the mountains, the seas, the plants, the animals, the fish, the birds, the planets and the stars are constantly praising God, not consciously as we do, but simply by virtue of fulfilling the purposes for which they have been created. Scientists tell us that the stars in the heavens are continually singing in concert. Although stellar sound waves cannot be heard by the human ear, they can be detected with specialized telescopes. Perhaps stellar vibrations are their way of fulfilling the first commandment: to love God. The sun and the other stars fulfil the second commandment of loving their neighbours by providing us with light and heat.

Your voice can give clarity and consciousness to their praise. You can thank the Father for the love with which he has fashioned the galaxies, comets, meteors and planets. You can praise the Father for the warmth and light of the sun during the daytime and the light of the moon and stars by night. You can glorify the Father for the blue sky, the air, the winds, the clouds, the raindrops and the snowflakes. You can rejoice with the Father over the delicacy of the morning dew and the moonbeams, over the intricate design of every insect, leaf, and flower. You can be the angel singing to God on behalf of all creation. There is a stirring quotation attributed to the *Talmud* that goes like this: 'Every blade of grass has its angel that bends over it and whispers, "Grow, grow"'.

Third, join your voice to those of the saints and angels who are constantly praising God in heaven. There are saints you know, and those of whose sanctity you are unaware, among them your ancestors, relatives and friends.

Include others in this prayer by saying the first word of the Lord's Prayer, the word 'our', in a deliberate and an intentional way. When you say 'Our Father', the entire world can be present in this single word 'our', as long as it truly surges from your heart. The entire world embraces so much and so many – those now on this planet, those who have gone before you and those who will come after you, and not just human beings, but all of creation, including the birds of the air, the beasts of the fields, the flowers of the meadows, the highest mountains and the deepest valleys, and even the stars in the most distant galaxies. You can gather up all of creation in your prayers because you are body and soul, visible and invisible. You unite in yourself the two basic poles of life – the material and the spiritual – and so you can bring both before God in adoration.

As well as never praying alone, it does not make sense just to pray for yourself. God is neither my God nor your God. God is *our* Father. When you pray for others, your prayer has a much bigger impact. You've probably heard of the butterfly effect, the idea that a single tiny act like a butterfly flapping its wings can have a huge impact, eventually leading to winds that generate a tornado. Something minor can have major consequences: a single bat apparently transmitting a virus to a person in Wuhan, China, brought the whole world to its knees. We tend to think that powerful leaders or massive wars or huge earthquakes are what change the world. But the truth is that the world is changed by the tiniest of things – whether it's a butterfly flapping its wings or a man eating the flesh of a bat. The world is also changed for the good in the smallest of ways – for example, by a person quietly praying the Our Father.

Not only are we all interconnected with each other, but we're all connected to the Father. He is the Father of us all.

Father, help each of us to find a place within this tiny word 'our', a place large enough for each of our stories, for each of our loves, and for all of our lives. Help us to believe how precious we are in your sight, so precious that even the very hairs of our head are numbered. Give us the grace to trust that your love for us revealed in Jesus is a love without limits. Amen.

Father
Three figures emerge from the ruins of a burning city – three men spanning three generations, and all (literally) linked together. Most

visible is a man in the prime of life. He carries his elderly father on his back. Walking at his side is his small son whom he holds by the hand. And all the while, the man keeps looking back to be sure that his wife is walking safely behind the three of them. This is the most iconic scene in Virgil's masterpiece, the *Aeneid*. The strong man is Aeneas, a father who is fully committed to the care of his family. The burning city is Troy, a city that has been sacked and destroyed. But the chaos of the crumbling city doesn't deter Aeneas. This man of courage and resilience guides his family safely away from the devastation of war. A loving father, Aeneas places the life of his little son above his own interests. The labour of love does not wear him down. The selfless love of Aeneas is an image of the love of the Eternal Father.

Today, many children would dearly love to have a father of the quality of Aeneas. There are children who don't even know who their fathers are. At times they have no more than a fleeting acquaintance with their biological fathers, who disappear during their childhood and are not present to help them mature. But even when fathers play an important role in their development, at times they remain puzzling and remote figures. Grown-up children don't always find it easy to understand their dads. They find it hard to draw close to them. They are often at a loss to say who their fathers really are. They have little or no idea of the inner lives of these men, of what they think and feel. And yet, appreciating their own fathers for who they are is important. It is especially important for the sons of these fathers. Until they come to see their own fathers more clearly, both in terms of their virtues and their flaws, most men will find it difficult to find the right balance in being fathers themselves. They will either become such strong fathers that they will be tempted to deny freedom to their children, or they will become so weak that they will offer them no real protection.

The good news is that men have more than one chance to have a father. Life provides father figures in many different guises – relatives, teachers and work colleagues can all serve as mentors. Ultimately, God himself can be the father that we lacked as children.

God has a clear advantage over human fathers, and that advantage is not just extensive practice but eternal experience! Men become fathers when they have children. Before they have children, they aren't fathers. What is fascinating about God is that he didn't start being a father at a certain point in time – he has always been a Father, because he has always had a Son. In the case of God's relationship with creation, things are different: there was a time when God hadn't created the world, and so he only became Creator once he brought creation into being. In other words, Father is a title that has always been held by God, whereas Creator is not. Or to put it differently, fatherhood is the core and eternal identity of one of the three persons of the Blessed Trinity.

Before the time of Jesus, nobody would have guessed that there are three persons in the same God. It was only when Jesus revealed himself as the Son of the Father that people began to sense there might be more to this one God than they had imagined. Jesus never denied the Jewish belief in a single God. But although conserving belief in God as one and unique, his words gradually helped his disciples see that this single God comprised more than one person. In order to explain who he was, Jesus liked to speak of the Father: 'the Father has sent me' (Jn 20:21). During the Last Supper, he explained that another divine person – the Holy Spirit – would descend upon the disciples to enable them to understand his teaching. On the basis of what Jesus taught, believers began to realise that there were three persons in this one God.

Jesus explains that he is completely dependent on the Father, doing nothing of himself. He says that he imitates the Father in everything, only doing 'what he sees the Father doing' (Jn 5:19). He makes it clear that there is an unfathomable bond of love between the Father and himself, 'The Father loves the Son' (Jn 5:20). Jesus makes it clear that he doesn't live for success but for the Father: 'I seek to do not my own will but the will of him who sent me' (Jn 5:30).

There are a number of references to God's fatherhood in the Hebrew scriptures. God is also called father in several Jewish prayers. But Jesus, as the only begotten Son of the Father, gives an experiential depth to this Jewish understanding of God's father-hood that is truly extraordinary. This is because Jesus is, always has been, and always will be, the Son of the Father. Although we have fathers, sooner or later they disappear from the scene – when we grow up and move out of home, and sometimes even sooner. Eventually our fathers die, and although we may be left with good memories, these are still only memories. But there is an eternal 'nowness' about Jesus' relationship to his Father: the Father is always generating him as his Son, giving him all of himself, and the Son is always returning all of his love to the Father. This love is so powerful that it is the third person of the Blessed Trinity, the Holy Spirit.

In many world religions, God is so majestic that believers feel he couldn't possibly descend to the familiar level of being a Dad. And there is something accurate about this feeling of how unlikely it is, because it truly is astounding that God would even want to be on such intimate and familial terms with us. Similar to believers from many other faiths, we Christians believe in God's utter supremacy. Yet at the same time, we dare to address this supreme Lord of the universe as 'Father'.

If we find ourselves saying the words 'Our Father' without a second thought, something is wrong: the immensity of the gift of being able to call God by this title has not yet dawned upon us. We would never have dared to do so had Jesus not invited us to be so audacious. In fact, Jesus has not just invited us to call God by this name; he has won this privilege for us.

Jesus shows us that God is tender as well as transcendent. It's difficult for us to honour the intimacy that God offers us while also respecting his immensity: we tend to exaggerate one at the expense of the other. We either think of him as so heavenly that he becomes a distant figure, or as so close that he becomes a bland buddy.

Father, the depth of your wisdom and knowledge are beyond my ability to grasp. How unsearchable are your judgments and how inscrutable your ways! For who could know your mind or be your counsellor? And yet you are so near each one of us. For in you we live and move and have our being. We are your children.

From God to Father

In the West, more and more people view God as an impersonal force who is not involved in their lives. Many people never go beyond this notion of a distant God. They never take the leap of faith necessary to view God as a loving Father. Even when they do believe that God is somehow connected with their lives, they are tempted to see him as a controlling or unwelcome force.

Many Christians view God in a poor light as well. Some find it hard to trust him, afraid that he has misery and misfortune in store for them. Others feel they are in a one-sided relationship with God; they do their bit but God never gives them what they ask for and need. Even apparently positive images of God can turn sour; some Christians start with an image of God waving his wand to make things better, but as time goes by, and they come to encounter the difficult realities of suffering and evil, they wonder why this magician in the sky doesn't wave his wand more often.

Many of these negative pictures of God can be traced back to childhood experiences. A boy who experiences little warmth from his stern and distant father may end up with a distorted image of a severe and punishing God. A girl who never feels good enough to please her impossibly demanding mother may grow up with an image of God as the eternally displeased one who is always wagging his finger at her.

We are all tempted to cling on to immature images of God. As adults we may proclaim our faith in an unconditionally loving God; yet in moments of panic we can find ourselves reverting to a childish and fearful image of God as someone who has it in for us.

Childish views of God are often magical: we think that if we use the right formula, we'll manage to get what we want. When we view God in a magical way, we are not really ready to worship him. Instead, whether we own up to it or not, we are really setting out to manipulate him. As we grow up in our faith, we move from magic to mystery. We begin to sense that God is too deep to be manipulated and too vast to be controlled. When we recognise the mystery of God, we're ready to worship God in spirit and in truth.

If you picture God as strict and angry, you'll want to keep your distance, but if you keep your distance, your relationship with him will never grow, and you'll never discover what a wonderful Father God is. You need to go beyond the strict policeman god, the stern, judgemental god and the demanding schoolteacher god.

It helps to nourish your image of the heavenly Father from the best available images of human fatherhood. Perhaps you can picture Aeneas in Virgil's *Aeneid*. Maybe it's easier to draw on real-life images closer to home. Just imagine a human father holding his baby for the first time, moments after his wife gives birth to their child. Picture this strong father, holding that baby with tremendous love and tenderness. The extraordinary warmth and love of a human father with his new-born child is just a pale image of the warmth and love of our heavenly Father.

We associate Jesus with kindness, love and affection. Yet we over-look the fact that the Father is exactly like Jesus in these respects. As the Letter to the Hebrews tells us in Chapter 1, verse 3, Jesus is the very radiance of the Father's glory and the express image of his person, or as Jesus tells us in the Gospel of John, 'the Father and I are one' (Jn 10:30).

We are inclined to think of the Father as cold, distant and unin-terested. The truth is that the Father loves us with a love we cannot even begin to fathom. The truth is that the Father really wants to be known and loved by us. Even if our sins are red as scarlet, the Father will forgive us if only we turn to him and tell him we're sorry and we want to change. He will make us white as snow. All we need is to approach the Father with confidence and love. Our trust and our love will make God forget our sins.

God is a Father who so wants to forgive us. We can see this huge desire of God in the parable of the Prodigal Son, also called the story of the Loving Father: 'But while he was still far off, his father saw him and was filled with compassion; he ran and put his arms around him and kissed him' (Lk 15:20).

All of us know how much a mother is willing to forgive the sins and failings of her children. The love of God the Father for each of us is more tender than the love of any mother for her child. As

God says through the mouth of the prophet Isaiah, 'Can a woman forget her nursing child or show no compassion for the child of her womb? Even these might forget, yet I will not forget you' (Isa 49:15). All we need to do is to call the Father by name, say 'Our Father' with trust, confidence and love, and we will receive the Father's love and mercy in return. There have been saints so convinced of the Father's infinite love that they have wanted to stand on all the rooftops of the world and cry out: 'the Father is love, the Father is love, the Father is love!'

We're grateful to someone who does us a favour. The Father has done us a massive favour. Not only has he given us life, he has also created us in his own image. God has given each of us a heart that can love in imitation of his great love. God more than deserves our love and veneration. God is a Father in whom we can have unlimited confidence. If you're a child of this kind of Father, it's easy to be trusting, candid and carefree. You are not weighed down by your cares. You don't need to dwell on your problems. You don't feel compelled to nurse grudges. You can hope for happy endings, because you know that God will take care of everything.

Our Father, your love is more tender than the love of the best mother in the world. I need to remind myself of this truth again and again. If I can only allow this truth to seep into my heart, my very life will be transformed. Father, with you in my life, I've nothing to fear. Instead, I've every reason to rejoice. Help me to recognize and celebrate your infinite love and goodness toward me and toward everyone.

Abba Father

There is one place in the Gospels where Jesus uses two words together that both mean 'father'. In the Gospel of Mark, when Jesus is praying in the Garden of Gethsemane, he feels the full awfulness of his impending suffering. At this moment of intense agony and struggle, Jesus says, 'Abba Father' (Mk 14:36). He asks the Father to take the cup away from him. Jesus adds that the Father's will, not his, should be done.

'*Abba*' is an Aramaic word for Father, and expresses a deep sense of intimacy, confidence and affection. Why does the Gospel of

Mark combine this Aramaic word for father (*Abba*) with the Greek word for Father (*pater*)? Perhaps in order to make us doubly sure of how genuine God's fatherhood is. In our Gethsemane moments we need to be more than certain of God's astonishing love.

This *Abba* relationship was so deep that at the most difficult moment of all, Jesus still went forward. He wasn't immobilised by fear. He trusted the Father. He knew that the Father loved him more than was humanly possible.

A father who is *Abba* is much more than a biological father. He is someone who cares enormously. He is someone who gives spiritual as well as material nourishment. He is someone that a child can turn to with straightforward and total trust. *Abba* Father's love is not only tender, it is also tremendously strong.

The Hebrew Bible or Old Testament often expresses God's tenderness with two Hebrew words that suggest the double nature of the Father's love – both masculine and feminine. The first word, '*hesed*', is fatherly in tone. '*Hesed*' conveys God's loving kindness, his enduring mercy, his unconditional loyalty and his utter faithfulness. The second word, '*racham*', is motherly in quality. '*Racham*' expresses the kind of heartfelt and tender compassion a mother has for her infant child. '*Racham*' is always used to describe God's love reaching out to those who are wounded or cut off in some way, bringing them back into a warm relationship. '*Racham*' has maternal roots: this word apparently comes from a similar-sounding Hebrew word '*rechem*', which means womb. In the Book of the Prophet Isaiah, God expresses his exquisite tenderness using both of these Hebrew words for love: 'In a surge of anger I hid my face from you for a moment, but with everlasting kindness [*hesed*] I will have compassion [*racham*] on you' (Isa 54:8).

Even when we say we believe in God's love, this faith can still remain only in our heads: our hearts and feelings can lag far behind. We find it challenging to believe in the God who believed enough in us to lay down his life for us. We find it demanding to live for the God who lived for us. We find it difficult to keep seeking the God who never stops seeking us.

Perhaps this is a hangover from our imperfect, earthly fathers. It is not always easy to love human fathers. If children feel abandoned by their father, resentment easily follows: they wanted him to be part of their lives, but he wasn't. Even though he may have been living at home, his career ended up taking up most of his time and energy. Others were hurt by their father at vulnerable moments in their lives, just when they most needed his support. Or perhaps they began to dislike their father when they saw him hurting their mother. Whatever the reason, children, whether young or grown-up, can feel hurt by their fathers.

Even if your father is a wonderful father, there will always be something lacking. Perhaps what is lacking is a perfect relationship with him. And because of the limitedness of your father or the limits of your relationship with him, your image of fatherhood is no doubt limited in some way or other.

The problem is that our own image of an imperfect human father can have a negative effect on our image of God the Father. Dislike of human fathers easily translates into dislike of the heavenly Father. Or sometimes we can project our image of some other father figure onto God. For example, if we've had a severe schoolteacher or if we have had to appear in court before a strict judge, we can wrongly imagine that God is like them; we can wrongly suppose that God is tough and judgemental.

We need the power of the Spirit to believe that God really is our *Abba* Father, someone we can approach with unlimited confidence. That is why St Paul tells us in the Letter to the Romans that God has placed the Spirit of Jesus into our hearts, and it is through this very Spirit that Jesus cries out through us the same words he uttered in the Garden of Gethsemane: 'Abba Father!'

St Thérèse of Lisieux was full of the Spirit of Jesus. That is why she could say that even if she had committed the worst possible crimes, she would lose none of her confidence. She would simply throw herself into God's arms, totally trusting in his mercy and love. Thérèse knew in her heart (and not only in her head) that God the Father is infinitely kinder, infinitely more loving and infinitely more tender than any human father. There is a wonderful line in the

Catechism of the Catholic Church that confirms this: 'No one is father as God is Father' (239).

This line from the *Catechism* is not unlike something that Jesus says, 'call no one your father on earth, for you have one Father, the one in heaven' (Mt 23:9). Jesus is saying that human fathers are not fathers in the proper sense of the term. All those people we regard as fatherly are so in a limited way. True fatherhood is only found in God, and any other fatherhood we experience is only a pale reflection of God's fatherhood.

We need to ask the Holy Spirit to help us stop picturing the heavenly Father as a strict policeman, a stern judge or a demanding schoolteacher. Just bring to mind for a moment the best human father you can possibly imagine. Now, could you agree that God is at least as good as this best human father? And could you take a much bigger step by granting that God is immensely, even infinitely, better than this best of human fathers? In other words, the extraordinary warmth of the best human father you can imagine actually pales in comparison with the tenderness and love of the real Heavenly Father.

God, Our Father, Jesus called you 'Abba Father'. Give me the Spirit of Jesus so that I can trust that you are the most tender of Fathers, with a tenderness beyond any tenderness I can imagine. I am sorry that I have distanced myself from you so often, because I wrongly pictured you as distant. You want to be so close to me, and to all of us. May your Holy Spirit help me recognize more and more what a wonderful and loving Father you are, so that I may grow in my love and affection for you. Amen.

Our True Selves: Children of God
Imagine you were to ask God, 'When do I bring you the most joy? When I do something well?'

How do you think he would respond? I would hazard a guess that God might respond like this, 'No, not when you do something well. The truth is, you bring me the most joy when you are a child, and that is when you are most yourself, because at the deepest level of your being you're not Irish or middle-class or intelligent or working or retired, you're a child of God.'

When we do things well, we tend to give ourselves a big pat on the back, but a child knows it cannot do anything by itself. A child brings its emptiness (and *not* its fullness!) to its father or mother. The child cries out, 'Help me, I can't manage on my own!' And that childlike spirit appeals to God, because it's the truth.

Each of us is a child of God. There are two layers of meaning to the expression 'child of God'. The first is our identity as children of God by virtue of being created, because God is the father of all of us. It is because God is the Father of all of humanity that Jesus died for each one of us. This means that the Holy Spirit is not only at work in the baptised, but in the hearts of all people of good will.

We were not born because we requested it. We were created by God without having asked to be created in advance. Once we developed and grew, we began to exercise our freedom of choice. God respects our free will, which means he doesn't force salvation upon us. Although God created us without any help of ours, he won't save us without our consent.

This brings us to the second layer of meaning in being children of God. It is up to us to choose freely this second dimension of being children of God. It is ushered in through baptism, which marks a new relationship with the Father, the Son and the Holy Spirit. Since many of us were baptised before we ourselves could make a free choice, we need to appropriate this gift of baptism by making a free choice for faith as adults.

Although our first birth happens without our consent, we cannot be born anew through water and the Holy Spirit without wanting it. We are free to choose or refuse this gift of new life. We choose it through a love that is free and not instinctual. This deeper reality of divine childhood makes it possible for us to grow spiritually, grounding ourselves in the love of the Father, the Son and the Holy Spirit.

In his Letter to the Romans (Rom 8:21), St Paul announces that we shall be delivered out of slavery into the glorious freedom of the children of God. Paul tells us that we shall be delivered – in other words, we cannot do it on our own. To arrive at this exhilarating freedom, we first need God's help to escape from the inner prison of our conflicted moods and dispositions. Left to ourselves, it's all too easy to get stuck at the level of our false self.

The false self is like the outer part of an onion that is wrapped in layers and layers of control, competitiveness and fear. The true self is at the centre of the onion, deep inside. The false self has its own peculiar ways of seeing reality, and does not open itself to other and better ways of seeing. It looks at people in terms of whether they will give pleasure or pain, security or insecurity, increased power or the loss of control. In *New Seeds of Contemplation*, Thomas Merton comments, 'There is no evil in anything created by God, nor can anything of his become an obstacle to our union with him. The obstacle is in our "self", that is to say, in the tenacious need to maintain our separate, external, egotistic will. It is when we refer all things to this outward and false "self" that we alienate ourselves from reality and from God. It is then the false self that is our god, and we love everything for the sake of this self.'

The false self seems to promise freedom. It appears to allow us to do what we want, where we want, when we want, and with whomever we want. In reality, its falseness enslaves us, because it places us at the mercy of our fears, hurts, anger and narcissism. Only through the power of the Spirit can we go deeper than this savage and sulking self to arrive at the self that can trust its feelings and be with others in a non-domineering and non-performing way.

Everlasting Father, how easy it is for me to lose confidence – a scowling face or a hurtful remark is enough to throw me into a foul humour. And it's strange how sometimes it's so easy for me to find confidence again – a radiant smile or a word of encouragement can light a flicker of resurrection. In the months and years ahead, I will get trapped many times by my false self. Thanks to your help, I also believe I will escape from its clutches again and again. When the darkness seems to settle over me, help me to trust that there can be light again, and that I can enter the glorious freedom of being your child.

The Soul – Sign of God's Fatherhood
The soul isn't a thing, so however powerful the microscope you use, you will never manage to see it. Neither can you grasp it; you may

as well try to get hold of a ray of sunlight. This invisible and intangible gem has definite qualities, however. These qualities are divine qualities – the soul is free, intelligent and continues to exist forever, just like God. This divine spark points to your identity as a child of God. It shows that you are created in the image and likeness of the Father.

If you have ever been with a loved one when they die, it's not hard to believe in the existence of the soul. Your loved one, whose voice, smile and expression were so dear to you, suddenly appears different and even strange. They look like a lifeless shell. When the animating principle of the body – the soul – is no longer there, the living person is reduced to a lifeless corpse.

Although the soul itself cannot be seen, it can be seen indirectly in many qualities that distinguish us from animals. Take language for instance. Animals communicate, and some even exchange messages in elaborate ways, but only human language uses sentences with subjects, verbs and objects – such as 'I love you' – and only human language employs the past, present and future tenses. Human language can focus on everything from concrete realities such as the person in front of me to abstract things such as the meaning of life.

A dog will remember its master and bark with delight when he returns home after a week away, but human memory can remember much more than particular things. My memory enables me to remember something larger and more vital. As well as remembering what I did in the past, I also remember that it was I who did these things. My memory helps me hold onto the past and in the process it helps me hold onto myself. A wonderful literary example of how a particular memory opens up to something much larger can be found in the first volume – *Swann's Way* – of Marcel Proust's *Remembrance of Things Past*. One winter's day, the narrator's mother gives him a cup of tea and a small sweet pastry called a 'petite Madeleine'. He soaks a morsel of the pastry in a spoonful of tea, and as he raises it to his lips and it touches his palate he shudders with pleasure at a memory from childhood. He remembers when he was a child that his aunt Léonie used to give him a petite Madeleine on

Sunday mornings after dipping the pastry in her own cup of tea. And with this particular memory, a whole series of memories flood into his mind: the old grey house where her room was, the village of Combray in which she lived, the streets he used to run along, the country roads he walked upon, the people of Combray, its life and surroundings.

The human imagination is immeasurably richer than the imagination of an animal. A dog that receives a bone each day is capable of imagining this bone even before the bone has been set down in front of it by its owner, but human beings can imagine things which are not there and have never existed, just as J.R.R. Tolkien imagined the extraordinary fantasy world of Middle-earth, where the events of *The Hobbit* and *The Lord of the Rings* unfold.

Because of the soul we have the courage and ability to love forever. An animal displays an instinctive love: a mother tiger will risk her life to protect its cubs, but will do nothing to defend the young offspring of another tiger. A human being can love in a conscious and intentional way, going beyond instinct. We can lay down our lives for our friends, or even for a stranger, as the Franciscan priest Maximilian Kolbe did in Auschwitz in July 1941, when he volunteered to be killed in place of a man who was married and had a family.

An animal can be physically majestic, but only a human being can grow beautiful in goodness, and this radiant goodness – clearly and compellingly visible in the face of someone like Mother Teresa of Calcutta – is a manifestation of the soul.

The soul enables us to enter into dialogue with God – a loving, free and living dialogue. It is because of this capacity for divine dialogue that the soul is immortal. The fact that each person has a soul – this divine spark or gem – means that each person is wanted and loved by God in a special way. Each one is called into an eternal dialogue with God.

This dialogue with God is not just any kind of conversation but a conversation of love. All love wants to last forever. God's love is so powerful that it not only wants eternity but makes eternity happen.

That is why we say that God is the God of the living and not of the dead. So, although we may feel fragile and small – 'poor potsherd' in the words of Gerard Manley Hopkins – each of us, in fact, is an 'immortal diamond'.

The soul, this immortal diamond, is beautiful because it is in God's image and likeness. Although everything God created is good, the soul shines with a magnificent beauty because it is so like him.

The soul is also a curious kind of diamond. When we think of diamonds, we usually picture smooth, polished, sparkling stones with a metallic lustre. But the soul is a special kind of diamond, because we cannot see it. It has a beauty that is invisible to our eyes, but no less real for that. After all, 'It is only with the heart that we truly see; what is essential is invisible to the eye' (Antoine de Saint-Exupéry). To bolster our belief in the reality of the soul, we need to remind ourselves that there are many real things which are invisible to our eyes. We cannot see wi-fi, air or electricity, but this invisibility does not make them any less real.

We need to use the imagination when it comes to the soul. To imagine does not mean to make something up; instead, it is about seeing with our mind's eye something that is not visible before our physical eyes. To imagine does not mean to escape reality, but instead to see reality in a bigger and better way.

We need to enlarge our vision of the soul by realising that God makes his home in the soul of a good person. This is mind-boggling, beyond our power to comprehend. Instead of trying to grasp it, we need to be grasped by it.

If we could allow this truth to take possession of us, we would do our utmost to preserve the heavenly beauty of the soul by making every effort not to disturb the radiance of this immortal diamond that shines in us and through us.

Love makes the soul into a 110-carat diamond. The only thing that wounds the soul and disfigures its beauty is doing evil. Socrates, the ancient Greek philosopher, was reputed to be physically ugly, but he was admired for a beauty that was more than skin-deep – the beauty of his soul. He prayed for inner beauty at the end of the *Phaedrus*. You could pray for beauty of the soul as well.

Heavenly Father,
I want outer beauty; give me inner beauty.
I hunger for love; may I feed on you.
I am satisfied with so little; help me to expect marvels.
I am dulled by routine; help me walk on the waves of wonder.

CHAPTER TWO

Who Art in Heaven

*Your sweet face is for me heaven on earth ... my only
homeland, it's my kingdom of love.*
St Thérèse of Lisieux

The Longing for Heaven

C.S. Lewis regarded heaven as a state of pure happiness. A state
beyond our grasp but not beyond our longing. We have inklings
of heaven, but ultimately these hints and clues disappoint us. As
Lewis remarked in his famous sermon 'The Weight of Glory', these
inklings are ultimately a let-down because they 'are not the thing
itself; they are only the scent of a flower we have not found, the
echo of a tune we have not heard, news from a country we have
never yet visited.'

Already as a small child, C. S. Lewis sensed an extraordinary
world beyond the ordinary. He knew there was something super-
natural beyond everything that seemed so natural and taken for
granted. One day his older brother Warren showed him a toy
garden he had made on the lid of a biscuit tin. For Lewis, this was
a golden moment. It was not the biscuit tin itself that awakened his
pang of longing. It was as though the toy garden on the biscuit tin
were the messenger of something else, something he could not put
his finger on, a sensation of beauty that lasted a moment, and then
vanished. In that moment, C. S. Lewis caught a glimpse of something that opened up a deep desire he had never known before, the
desire for his true homeland, heaven.

Many of us can resonate with C. S. Lewis here. At the most
unexpected moments, we've had a sense of the beyond. Without
knowing it, we may just have experienced God in the midst of our
everyday lives. We've been brought face to face with a desire deep

in our hearts that longs for a love beyond love, a happiness beyond happiness. Looking back at this childhood experience as an adult, C. S. Lewis wrote: 'As long as I live my imagination of Paradise will retain something of my brother's toy garden.' C. S. Lewis captures an important feature of heaven – although beyond our imagination, it is nevertheless our homeland. Since we are focusing on the Father, it might be appropriate to call it our fatherland, even more than our homeland.

It is the place where God is, and wherever God is, there is true love. Some of us have been lucky to spend time in the company of a noble and generous friend. Something in us wants to stay forever with that kind of person. In their company we no longer feel oppressed by the burden of suffering or the weight of evil. A single smile of a truly good person is enough to make everything appear more radiant. Their goodness is a small image of what heaven is like. Heaven only contains goodness, because God is there, and God is the source of all love.

When we pray 'Our Father, who art in heaven', we're also reminding ourselves to fix our gaze on this fatherland of ours. Who wants to be in exile forever? A soldier stationed abroad longs to return home. If heaven is our homeland, then it's natural to yearn to be there. There's nothing impersonal about heaven: our parents and grandparents, our friends and relatives await us there. It will be such a joy to meet them and embrace them once again.

Heaven is not made up of an endless and repetitive cycle of days, weeks, months and years. It is a moment so full that we can plunge completely into it, a moment of infinite love that is experienced always in a new way, and yet also always as though for the very first time.

The newness and delight of heaven are illuminated by a story about a medieval monk. The monk found it hard to become enthusiastic at the prospect of eternal happiness. He couldn't warm to the image of angels playing harps on fluffy clouds. One afternoon he walked deep into the forest. At a crossroads where two paths met, he stopped, captivated by the mellow sound of a blackbird in song. He stood there listening for a long time. When he returned to the monastery, nothing looked familiar. He didn't recognise the monks, and they had no idea who he was. He asked to see the abbot. But when he gave the abbot's name, the monks looked at him in utter amazement: this abbot had died a hundred years before!

This legend gives us an inkling of what heaven is like. Heaven is a moment so full that all of time seems to have been absorbed into it: heaven is the eternal now. The present moment is where eternity and time embrace each other. God waits for us in this precise moment. We distract ourselves from the present through replaying the past or anticipating the future. Yet we are only ever in the present moment. We are not in the future, and we are not in the past. This present moment is omnipresent, because we are never in time gone by or time yet to come, but only in the now. The now is omnipresent, just as God is, because God is present in all time; for God, all time is the eternal now. The more we surrender ourselves to the now of the present moment, the closer we get to God.

Father, forgive me for my petty desires and puny dreams. As though I were only destined for dust and ashes, whereas all the while you want me to turn right at Orion and dance among the stars. I've lost sight of my greatness in a flood of drivel. I've lost my sense of heaven in a buzz of silly criticisms and stupid compromises. Help me to dream again as though I were dreaming for the first time.

Getting Beyond a Vague Sense of Heaven

The Père Lachaise cemetery in Paris must be one of the most visited graveyards in the world. A number of years ago I had the opportunity to explore this cemetery that contains the mortal remains of so many celebrities. I remember stopping at the burial site of Frédéric Chopin. Although Chopin's heart was returned to his native Poland, his body was placed in this large Parisian cemetery. Bunches of fresh flowers surrounded the enormous tombstone, and perched on top was the statue of a distraught woman representing the muse of music. Oscar Wilde's tomb, which took almost a year to sculpt, drew many tourists. Less ornate than Chopin's and Wilde's, but even more popular with sightseers, was the tombstone of the singer Jim Morrison.

Why do people spend so much money (Oscar Wilde's tomb alone cost 2,000 pounds, and that was in the early years of the last century) and expend so much energy in decorating the graves of relatives and friends? Would they do so if they believed that their cherished ones had simply disintegrated, turned into dust and become food for worms? They dare to believe these loved ones are still alive in a way they cannot quite comprehend; somehow, they hope that death hasn't had the last word. And why is it that when people visit graveyards, they often find themselves speaking in their hearts with their buried relatives? Because they believe these relatives are not definitively beyond the reach of life.

Even though people often feel a bond with loved ones who have died, they don't move from these feelings to clear thoughts about the afterlife: they don't think much about what life after death could possibly mean. They only have a vague sense of the afterlife. However, if we give thought to life after death, it might just become easier to believe that God, who gives us life in the first place, has the power to bring us back to life once again. We might just grow in confidence that our physical death is *not* the end of our human existence.

Listening to the everyday comments people make about heaven, it is striking that many picture it either as somewhat worse than earth – singing boring hymns without end – or as rather better – enjoying days full of endless sunshine. In these images something changes: our present experience either deteriorates or improves. These images miss out on what is essential about heaven. Paradise does not entail a change from life on earth; it involves a complete transformation. Change means enjoying a bigger (or smaller) quantity of the things we liked on earth; transformation means a quantum leap, a total shift of horizons. The real heaven is such an experience of bliss and delight that all our happiness in this world will appear fake and counterfeit by comparison.

We need more than a vague sense of the hereafter. We need to trust in heaven with all our hearts. Heaven provides us with a goal and destination to our lives. Having a worthwhile goal makes a huge difference.

The following story illustrates this point: long ago, toward the end of the twelfth century, a man was travelling through France. He came across three young apprentices to a stone-cutter. They were using long wooden sticks or levers to move enormous cut stones up a ramp. Turning to the first apprentice, the man asked, 'What are you doing?' The apprentice replied with an annoyed expression, 'Can't you see? I'm moving these stones up the ramp'. He then asked the second apprentice, who seemed a little more animated, 'What are you doing?' The second apprentice replied with a shrug of his shoulder, 'I'm just building a wall'. The man was really taken with the winning smile he noticed on the third apprentice's face, and he asked him, 'What about you, what are *you* doing?' The apprentice beamed, 'I'm building a cathedral'.

If you see yourself as simply moving a stone from one place to another, you won't get a lot of satisfaction. But if you have a great goal like heaven before your eyes, it makes an enormous difference: you will experience a sense of fulfilment, even now. The reality of heaven is a guarantee that even though one day you may be buried in a grave, you won't stay there. You are intended for something immeasurably greater than dust and ashes.

To prepare yourself well for heaven, you must love as much as you can and eliminate hatred from your life. As a concrete way of seeing if you are ticking the right boxes in your life, you can ask yourself if you are carrying out at least some of the corporal and spiritual works of mercy: feeding the hungry, clothing the naked, sheltering the homeless, visiting the sick, visiting the imprisoned, burying the dead, counselling the doubtful, instructing the ignorant, admonishing sinners, consoling the afflicted, pardoning offences, patiently putting up with difficult people, praying for the living and the dead. Each evening, it makes sense to look back prayerfully upon the day, asking yourself if you have practiced one or more of these works of mercy.

This may sound daunting. How can you manage it? Many holy men and women have found an easy way. They credit the Virgin Mary with getting them to heaven. Jesus came down to us through Mary, and Jesus would like us to come to him through her.

Mary is the gate to heaven. No wonder we always conclude the Hail Mary Prayer with this request: 'pray for us sinners now and at the hour of our death'. That most underrated of men, St Joseph, also plays an important role. Tradition has it that Joseph died in the arms of Jesus and of the Blessed Virgin Mary.

O Blessed Joseph, you breathed your last breath in the arms of Jesus and Mary. Obtain for me this grace, O holy Joseph, that I may breathe forth my soul in praise, saying in spirit, if I am unable to do so in words: 'Jesus, Mary and Joseph, I give you my heart and my soul. Amen.'

Heaven Isn't Far Away

The heavenly Father is more loving than any earthly father could possibly be and more real than anything else we take for real. But the words 'who art in heaven' seem to suggest that he is far away and somehow less real. How can you re-set your spiritual 'Global Positioning System' (GPS) so that heaven appears closer and more real?

Perhaps a (true) story will help. A friend of mine considered becoming a Carthusian monk. Since there is no monastery of Carthusian monks in Ireland, he spent several weeks in the Carthusian monastery in Parkminster, Sussex, England. Carthusians basically live as hermits and only gather together on certain occasions. They talk with each other just once a week when the whole community goes for a walk. Otherwise, they're pretty much immersed in silence and solitude.

Anyhow, before he finished his stay in the monastery, this friend had the opportunity to talk for a few minutes with one of the monks. My friend explained that he was afraid that when he returned to his busy life in the world, he wouldn't be able to stay faithful to the spirit of prayer he had absorbed in the cloister. He asked the monk for advice. This holy monk gazed at him with his radiant eyes for a long moment, and then uttered four words: 'Pray in, not up'. My friend was disappointed at the brevity of this reply. He felt he had poured out his soul, and all the monk said in response was, 'Pray in, not up'. But over time he began to see the wisdom of these words.

I guess we could put this monk's words as follows, 'Go in, not out'. And that's exactly the wisdom that is in the Lord's Prayer: 'who art in heaven'. Certainly, God is everywhere. But we tend to picture God as being somewhere else than where we are now, as being elsewhere, as being up there. The Carthusian monk was pointing out that God is in our hearts, so we can pray inwards. We don't need to spend all our time gazing upwards; instead, we can gather ourselves and turn our gaze to the God who is already within.

When we pray the words 'who art in heaven', we're not praying to a God who is far away. We're not addressing our words to someone who is in a distant place; instead, we're speaking to a Father whose majesty and might are beyond anything we can imagine. Heaven, in other words, is about God's way of being. God is utterly magnificent and breath-taking in his way of being. The *Catechism of the Catholic Church* makes pretty much the same point:

'This biblical expression ["who art in heaven"] does not mean a place ("space"), but a way of being; it does not mean that God is distant, but majestic. Our Father is not "elsewhere": he transcends everything we can conceive of his holiness. It is precisely because he is thrice holy that he is so close to the humble and contrite heart. "Our Father who art in heaven" is rightly understood to mean that God is in the hearts of the just, as in his holy temple' (*Catechism of the Catholic Church*, 2794).

Since heaven is a way of being, it can also become our way of being. If we lead upright and decent lives, God will dwell within us. God can manage to be marvellous, majestic, supreme, and still live in our hearts – remember, we're talking about God here! You might say, 'but I'm not worthy of this great God being present within me!' Well, who is worthy?! Our very unworthiness makes God's presence all the more astonishing an act of mercy and love.

Turn your gaze inwards, where God is dwelling inside you. As St Augustine famously said: 'God is closer to you than you are to yourself'. Less famously, but no less truly, St Augustine also said: 'Why climb the mountains or go through the valleys of the world looking for him who dwells within us?'

Of course, the realisation that God is present within us doesn't arrive instantaneously. We may 'know' it in our heads; but to experience it in our hearts – well, that's another thing. The thought that the transcendent, mighty, all-powerful God could be present within is mind-blowing. Nevertheless, some people arrive at this deep sense of God's presence. The great French mystic St Elizabeth of the Trinity declared, 'I have found my heaven on earth, because heaven is God, and God is in my heart.'

Our Father who art in heaven, how amazing that you make your dwelling within me. It sounds so extraordinary that I honestly have trouble even imagining that it could be possible. Help me to waken up to the rich reality of your presence. Help me to believe in this heaven within, that I may be filled with wonder, and live with something of the love and generosity of your Son Jesus Christ Our Lord. Amen.

CHAPTER THREE

Hallowed Be Thy Name

Do not be afraid of holiness. It will take away
none of your energy, vitality or joy.
Pope Francis

Encountering Holiness

We have now arrived at the first petition in the Lord's Prayer: 'hallowed be thy name'. God's name is already holy; in this petition we're asking that it be holy for us and in our lives.

During the long summers of childhood, I often wandered into a wild field near our house, where tall grass grew freely. I would flatten the lush grass and lie down on this thick carpet. From that luxurious bed, I used to gaze up at the blue sky above, and at the clouds slowly moving across its vastness. The immensity of the sky above made me feel thoroughly small by contrast. I was filled with a sense of awe at the majesty and grandeur of God.

This childhood experience was an encounter with holiness. When we speak of holiness, we often refer to moral goodness, but the primary meaning of holiness in the Bible is otherness or separateness. When the Bible talks about holiness, it is not focusing on morally perfect people. Instead, holiness is associated above all with God, and when biblical figures call God holy, they're saying that he is different from us and 'other' than us. The realm of the holy is the realm of the sacred, which is different from the profane. As a child, that place in the field was a place apart, a place where I experienced life in a different way than in the humdrum of daily routine.

We all have holy places – spaces where we experience a rhythm that is different from everyday life, where we quieten down to a pace that pacifies us. It might be something as simple as going for a walk through the neighbourhood at the end of a working day or standing in front of a blossoming flower and just savouring the moment.

As well as holy places, there are also holy times. Christmas is a holy time because it celebrates Christ's birth, and many of the customs and traditions around Christmas serve to distinguish this sacred time from ordinary time. First of all, Christmas itself is a big 'holiday', a word which comes from 'holy day'. And it is set apart from the rest of the year by everything from festive lights and decorations to Christmas carols and dinner with turkey and ham.

When I suggested that you choose a fitting place and time to pray, I was implicitly inviting you to create a holy place and holy time in your day, a space and time to help you enter into the 'otherness' of prayer.

What I've described so far are encounters with a limited kind of holiness. However, God is holy in an unrestricted way. At times we forget God's holiness and make him into such a harmless figure that we forget how mysterious and powerful he really is. We need to recover a sense of awe in the face of the utter mystery of God.

In a famous work from the early twentieth century, *The Idea of the Holy*, the German scholar Rudolf Otto famously described the encounter with holiness as an ambivalent experience. On the one hand, we are hugely attracted by holiness; on the other hand, it frightens us. As a result, God's holiness is a mystery that both draws us and frightens us, a terrifying and fascinating mystery: a *mysterium tremendum et fascinans*.

The holiness of God doesn't inspire the usual kind of fear. If you're confronted by an aggressive man wielding a stick, a burst of adrenaline will give you the extra injection of energy you need for fight or flight. But a strong sense of awe before God could keep you rooted to the spot and send a chill down your spine. You not only sense the greatness of God, but you also get a sudden and sharp sense of your own creatureliness. This kind of experience can leave you immobile and at a loss for words.

The holiness of God is not only daunting; it is also captivating. Encountering God's holiness takes you outside of yourself and also brings you back to yourself. It's ecstatic in the root meaning of the word: *ex-stasis*, a standing outside of yourself. And yet, although you're no longer self-absorbed, you also feel grounded as though you have finally come home to yourself.

Father, my soul bows to the ground, the holy ground deep within, where you are present. Help me to be still and silent, so that I may become wholly yours, and holy in your presence.

Isaiah's Vision of God's Holiness

There is a marvellous example of the impact of God's holiness early in the Book of the Prophet Isaiah. Incidentally, this passage from Isaiah is also an excellent illustration of how to prepare well for prayer, by adopting the threefold gaze of looking at God, ourselves, and the world around us.

This vision was granted to Isaiah at a time of huge national upheaval. King Uzziah had reigned for more than fifty years. For most of that time he had been a good, and even great, king. But as he grew more and more powerful, he also became increasingly proud, and pride turned out to be his undoing. Uzziah was struck with leprosy and died an outcast. With Uzziah's death, there was unease about what the future held.

In the midst of this unstable situation where there was no secure foothold, a prophet nevertheless found his calling. Isaiah had a momentous experience in the Temple that helped him become one of the greatest prophets in Jewish history.

In the year that King Uzziah died, I saw the Lord sitting on a throne, high and lofty, and the hem of his robe filled the temple. Seraphs were in attendance above him; each had six wings: with two they covered their faces, and with two they covered their feet, and with two they flew. And one called to another and said,

'Holy, holy, holy is the Lord of hosts;
the whole earth is full of his glory.'

The pivots on the thresholds shook at the voices of those who called, and the house filled with smoke. And I said, 'Woe is me! I am lost, for I am a man of unclean lips, and I live among a people of unclean lips, yet my eyes have seen the King, the Lord of hosts!'

Then one of the seraphs flew to me, holding a live coal that had been taken from the altar with a pair of tongs. The seraph touched my mouth with it and said, 'Now that this has touched your lips, your guilt has departed and your sin is blotted out.' Then I heard the voice of the Lord saying, 'Whom shall I send, and who will go for us?' And I said, 'Here am I; send me!' (Isa 6:1–8)

First of all, Isaiah's gaze is drawn by the majesty of God. Then he becomes aware of his own inadequacy. Finally, he volunteers to help others.

Let's begin with Isaiah's description of how he saw the Lord, high and lifted up. The Hebrew word used here for 'Lord' is *Adonai*. In the Bible this is a title of reverence for God, meaning a master or ruler with power and authority. Ironically, although Isaiah tells us that he saw the Lord, everything else he says seems to suggest that he didn't see God at all! That's because when he gives us the details of his vision, Isaiah doesn't so much speak about the Lord himself as about various items that made a striking impression upon him: the throne, the huge train, the seraphim, the smoke and the shaking of the Temple. The absence of any description of God is already a way of emphasising God's holiness. How can you describe the indescribable? God is so 'other' and so transcendent as to defy any description we can possibly provide.

The Lord is high, lifted up and seated on a throne, all signs of majesty and power. As for the train of the Lord's robe, it fills the Temple. We are accustomed to seeing long trains on royal wedding dresses. For her marriage in 1981 to Prince Charles, Princess Diana wore a wedding dress with a twenty-five-foot-long train. But the Lord's train is so large that there isn't space for anything else on the floor of the entire Temple. And that is just the train of his robe, not the robe itself!

The seraphim – which literally means 'fiery ones' – hover above God's throne, but this position does not mean they regard them-selves as superior to God. On the contrary, they cover their eyes

60

with two wings because the unveiled majesty of God is too powerful for them to endure. They cover their feet with two wings to bring everything they do under God's sway. They fly with two wings, showing that they are continually active in God's service. The seraphim, who burn because of their love for God, share some physical characteristics with human beings: they have faces, voices, hands and feet. They have such immense reverence for God that they dare not address him directly. Instead, they speak to each other about God's grandeur, proclaiming three times: 'holy, holy, holy'. They declare that the world is filled with his glory.

These words of the seraphim are full of power. When they proclaim God's holiness and the fact that the whole world is charged with his glory, the doorposts and thresholds of the Temple begin to shake and the entire building is engulfed in smoke. The threefold repetition of the word 'holy' brims with power and life. It is so full of life that it shakes the posts and thresholds.

There is nothing trivial about the holiness of God. In fact, God's holiness sets him apart as utterly unique. Although the seraphim are regarded as the highest of all angels, they are nevertheless much closer to us than they are to God. They are limited and created, just as we are. These celestial creatures are simply higher in the order of being than we are. The difference between the seraphim and ourselves is limited, but the chasm separating the seraphim from God is infinite. God is truly one of a kind.

Moreover, the seraphim declare that God's glory fills the earth. The seraphim are effectively inviting us to see the world in a new way. There are clear signs of chaos and carnage, of destruction and devastation in our world. These signs usually capture most of our attention. But the angels are telling us that underneath this surface reality there is something wondrous at work. God's plan is unfolding, and this plan is both brilliant and breath-taking.

Once he has witnessed something of the overpowering holiness of God, Isaiah's gaze turns toward himself. This is the second stage of the vision. Isaiah becomes aware of the contrast between God's majesty and his own unworthiness. The revelation of God's holiness exposes the reality of Isaiah's imperfection. Conscious of his own sinfulness, Isaiah fears that he may die as a result of what his eyes have seen.

Isaiah was probably a good and upright man. From a moral point of view, he may have stood out among his compatriots. But in comparison with God, Isaiah knew that he was practically nothing. The light of God's majesty reveals our own darkness. The greatness of God shows up our own littleness. The holiness of God exposes our own unholiness. It is only when we catch a glimpse of the reality of God that we begin to see ourselves as we truly are.

Isaiah cries out: 'Woe is me! I am lost'. There is a striking contrast between, on the one hand, the thundering commotion as the foundations of the Temple shudder; and, on the other hand, the solitary cry of this sinful man that follows. Even more striking is the fact that God, despite his greatness and majesty, deigns to respond to the faint-hearted Isaiah. In fact, God's response is immediate: without delay, a seraph flies toward Isaiah. The angel carries a burning coal from the altar. When this purifying coal touches Isaiah's lips, his guilt is removed. Crucially, Isaiah recognises his own inadequacy, and this honest acknowledgement of his neediness becomes the key that opens his life to service.

In Isaiah's vision, an angel cleansed the prophet's lips, but with the reality of the incarnation, it is God himself who comes among us, accomplishing our purification by his sacrifice of infinite love.

The gateway to service opens up in the third phase of the vision. At this point, Isaiah hears God's voice, full of concern for humanity, asking whom he can send. Isaiah, now filled with confidence because he has been cleansed, volunteers, 'Here I am, send me'. Isaiah's generosity is all the more remarkable because he still does not know what God actually wants him to do.

God's cleansing touch has obviously given Isaiah the freedom to see reality with new eyes. Freed of the burden of guilt and no longer preoccupied with himself, Isaiah's perspective has expanded beyond his own small world. He is ready to serve.

Father, when I contemplate your glory, I am filled with awe. In the face of your greatness, I feel small. In the face of your holiness, I feel sinful. But I also believe that your burning love can cleanse my heart. Touch me, heal me, and make me whole.

The Wonder of Adoration, Goodness and Mercy

We can refuse to adore God, but we cannot escape adoring someone or something. David Foster Wallace expressed this particularly well in his unforgettable commencement address at Kenyon College in 2005: 'In the day-to-day trenches of adult life, there is actually no such thing as atheism. There is no such thing as not worshipping. Everybody worships. The only choice we get is what to worship. And the compelling reason for maybe choosing some sort of god or spiritual-type thing to worship … is that pretty much anything else you worship will eat you alive.'

Alfred Delp, a German Jesuit priest, was executed by the Gestapo in February 1945, at the age of thirty-seven. During his imprisonment by the Nazis, he composed a meditation on the Our Father. He wrote, 'The God of life is a personal God and only when we enter into the dialogue with God do we begin to realize our dreams … Adoration is the road that leads us to ourselves.'

We could express Father Delp's final sentence in this way: hallowing God's name is the road that leads to ourselves. In the Bible, a person's name expresses the fullness of who they are, their deepest and most central identity. That's why when Jesus gave a new mission to Simon, he also gave him a new name, Peter. The Jewish people have traditionally shown such a huge reverence for God's name, that instead of pronouncing God's name, they simply refer to God as 'the Name' or in Hebrew *HaShem*.

How can we hallow, revere and treat as holy the name of the Father? By adoring him. Adoring God means being in awe before this God who lives and who loves, and who has given us life and who teaches us how to love. Adoration is the recognition of God's power and perfection and of our own complete reliance upon him.

St Elizabeth of the Trinity describes adoration in a lyrical and effusive manner. Adoration is 'an ecstasy of love. It is love overwhelmed by the beauty, the strength, the immense grandeur of the Beloved'. I only exist thanks to the love of God, who is love itself.

If I can begin to take in this marvellous reality, I'll want to kneel before this God who continues to show me such kindness and love.

From the beginnings of Christianity, Christians have traditionally followed a definite sequence in praying: first, adoration, then petitions. This sequence is a way of recognising that God's honour and God's interests come first – or in other words, hallowed be thy name.

Adoration is a huge interior reverence for God who is beautiful beyond any beauty we see in this world. His name is holier and more inviting than any other name. We give bodily expression to adoration by bowing, kneeling, laying on the ground, taking off our shoes … The gesture and reality of adoration are the beginning of true prayer.

Ultimately, adoration is love in its fullness. Adoration both recognises that we've received everything from God, and yearns to give everything to God in return. Adoration seeks to love God and to serve God in our lives and in our relationships. In other words, adoration aims directly at God through prayer, and indirectly through the way we relate to others.

That is why we also adore God and keep God's name holy by living lives of love. When we live as good people, God's name is hallowed in us. As Jesus puts it in the Gospel of Matthew: 'In the same way, let your light shine before others, so that they may see your good works and give glory to your Father in heaven' (Mt 5:16).

When we lead good lives, our lives point toward the absolute goodness and love of God, the One who is love itself, and so we are hallowing God's name.

This is what St Irenaeus was getting at when he said, 'The glory of God is the human being fully alive'. Our good actions are like beautiful songs or hymns that proclaim the greatness and glory of God.

One of the striking phrases of Pope Francis is, 'The name of God is mercy'. We hallow God's name in a particular way when we live God's infinite mercy in our lives. The roots of the Latin word for mercy – '*misericordia*' – tell us a lot. God has a heart that is sensitive to our pain and neediness; God has taken our *miseria* (misery) and

our pain into his *cordia* (heart). When we become merciful, the pain
of other people pains our hearts so much that we go to heartfelt
pains to relieve them.

Father, hallowed be thy name. Father, you are holy in everything.
Heal us of our blindness so that we may see and recognise and celebrate
your infinite love and goodness. Help us to re-shape our misshapen lives.
Give us a new vision of how our lives could be if we were friends to the
friendless, peacemakers to the troubled, voices of hope to those in despair,
and forces of forgiveness to those in need of mercy. May this new vision
and new way of living give you glory and hallow your name now and
forever. Amen.

Adoration Is Forever

Summer is traditionally the season when many priests are ordained,
and so it was for me. One of the most moving moments in the
whole ceremony was shortly before the moment of ordination itself,
when I lay flat on the floor, face down, head toward the altar, and
my hands, palms down, under my forehead.

I was positioned along the central aisle leading up to the high
altar of the Jesuit Church of St Francis Xavier in Gardiner Street,
Dublin. When you are lying prone with your face to the ground
just before ordination, it gives you a vivid sense of how small and
unworthy you are, and of how great God is. What makes lying on
the ground so encouraging is that the God before whom you are
prone is not a distant or uncaring God, but the God of all love.
Meanwhile, the congregation in the pews around you sings the
litany of the saints, and you feel supported and lifted up upon this
current of prayer. It's a stirringly sacred moment.

From the opening to the closing book of the Bible, human beings
repeatedly bow down in the presence of the All-Holy One, the only
One who truly is, the One who gives us our very life and being.
When God appears to Abram in Genesis 17, promising to make
a covenant with him, make him the father of many nations, and
change his name to Abraham, our father in faith falls face down
to the ground. Moses, for his part, bows down to the ground and
worships the God of the covenant in Exodus 34:8. In the Gospel

of Matthew 2:11, the Magi prostrate themselves on the ground and worship the infant Jesus. In Luke 5:12, a man covered with leprosy falls on his face before Jesus, imploring him, 'Lord, if you are willing, you can make me clean'. In Matthew 28:9, Mary of Magdala and the other Mary clasp the feet of the Risen Christ and worship him. In the Book of the Apocalypse 7:11, all the angels fall down on their faces before the throne and worship God. And most movingly of all, during his prayer in Gethsemane as his Passion began, we are told that Jesus himself 'threw himself to the ground and prayed' (Mt 26:39).

These biblical episodes show me that bowing down in adoration before God isn't merely a once in a lifetime gesture to be performed only at the threshold of priesthood. Instead, it makes sense to adopt a gesture of adoration whenever we come before the utter majesty of God. Getting down to the ground is something Muslims do all the time; their example reinforces the importance of this physical gesture. Prayer involves the whole person, and so it includes the body, and that's why the way we position our bodies during prayer shapes our very souls. Of course, it is the attitude of our minds and hearts that is most important in prayer. At the same time, we often forget how much bodily posture affects our hearts, our feelings and our entire attitude toward God. Bowing, kneeling and full prostration are three good ways of expressing our sense of worship and reverence in the presence of God.

To adore God is to place ourselves in God's presence, full of a deep sense of worship and love. To adore God is to recognise with gratitude that God has created us and is holding us in being right now. To adore God is to return to the very source of our lives, placing ourselves once again with trust and confidence in those loving hands from which we first came forth. Adoration is a matter of basic courtesy when it comes to God: without God, we wouldn't be here, and adoration is the humble acknowledgement of this fact. If we want to be courteous and polite, the best beginning is to make the most courteous gesture of all: to bow down in adoration before our Maker.

Before the greatness of God, I am next to nothing. Paradoxically, once I acknowledge this reality I end up unleashing enormous power. For if I can be humble in the face of God's majesty, then the combination of my littleness and God's greatness will form an incredibly potent mixture. The Virgin Mary knew her own littleness and God's greatness, and the Almighty truly worked marvels for her. For my part, I find there's always the temptation to rely on myself, even though I'm thoroughly unreliable. I'm repeatedly tempted to be proud, although I've nothing to be proud of, since all that I am and all that I have are gifts from God. Because of that recurrent temptation, I need to be brought back to earth (literally), through bowing down in adoration. As my fellow Jesuit Fr James Martin pleads at the end of his *New Serenity Prayer*, 'Basically God, grant me the wisdom to remember that I'm not you'.

Someday, when I finally step out of the shadows and the darkness into the light, it will dawn on me how truly tiny I really am, and I'll be astonished and overwhelmed with gratitude at God's goodness in reaching down to me, and blessing me in so many ways. In the meantime, I'm happy to adore God, and although I generally worship God through bowing and kneeling, sometimes adoration becomes even more real when I place my face on the ground and literally taste the dust from which I'm made.

Here I am before you Lord. I prostrate myself in your presence. During these moments of adoration, I leave aside everything that is not you: my cares and fears, my work and my hobbies. Like Mary of Lazarus, I want to choose the better part. I prefer to have a heart without thoughts than to have thoughts with no heart. I will become quiet so that I can hear you. I will listen to your silence, which speaks more eloquently than any words.

Chapter Four

Thy Kingdom Come

*If the Kingdom of God is in you, you should leave a
little bit of heaven wherever you go.*
Cornel West

The Kingdom Is a Mystery, Not a Problem

No one can offer an adequate definition of the kingdom of God,
and that's because God's kingdom is a mystery, and a mystery is
beyond definition. The Gospels themselves never provide us with a
definition of the kingdom. Jesus tells many stories and parables to
help us get a sense of what the kingdom is like. He never says that
any of these stories perfectly sum up the nature of the kingdom.
All he says is that the kingdom is 'like this' or 'similar to that'. The
kingdom is certainly mysterious.

Gabriel Marcel, the French philosopher, makes a helpful dis-
tinction between problems and mysteries. In life, we meet problems, and we also encounter mysteries. A problem is something
that is separate from you: a flat tyre in your bicycle, a Rubik's cube,
or a bug in your computer. To solve that problem, you use various
techniques. You try to master the problem, and mastering the problem involves distancing yourself from it so that you can examine
it thoroughly.

When it comes to a mystery, such as being in love, you cannot
separate yourself from it. This means that while you are reflecting
upon your love for someone, you are also reflecting upon yourself.
The mystery of being in love is not outside you, and not something
you solve; it is something you live.

Jesus says several times that the kingdom of God is near. Jesus
also says that the kingdom of God is within you (Lk 17:21).
Because it is within you, it is impossible to place it in front of you
as you might with a book or a laptop. The kingdom lights up your

life, but you cannot put it under the spotlight in such a way as to explain every aspect of it.

The central reason why the kingdom of God is so mysterious is because it is above all about the rule of a person – the Word made flesh, the person known as Jesus of Nazareth. If the kingdom of God is detached from Jesus, it is reduced to the problem of becoming better human beings, rather than the mystery of becoming true children of God. We see many examples of mysteries reduced to problems, everything from love reduced to sex to persons reduced to their DNA.

With the coming of Jesus, the absoluteness of God takes on human flesh and enters human history. This event is unheard of, completely new, a radical departure in human history. The kingdom of God is ushered in by this totally new beginning.

Since Jesus is fully human and fully divine, this means that when Jesus reigns in your life, there will be a perfect marriage between humanity and divinity. You become perfectly attuned to the divine ground of all things. The bond between God and humanity disintegrated with the Fall of Adam and Eve. The restoration comes with Jesus. Although Jesus embodies this new unity, it has not yet become a reality for many human beings, and for this reason the kingdom, although it has come with Jesus, still has to come for the rest of us. This is why we can say that the kingdom is both already here and yet still to come.

Any human kingdom, however large, has limits. Even if it embraces the whole world, a human kingdom is still limited by the limits of the earth. God's kingdom is without limits. It is a kingdom without borders or boundaries, precisely because it is the kingdom of *God*. This unlimited nature of God's kingdom means that it will always be a mystery to our eyes. However great we imagine it to be, it will always be greater than anything we can imagine.

Because God's kingdom is without limits, there is no limit to what God can do through us. The only limit is the limit we impose through our lack of trust and confidence in God.

Father, could I ever really speak to you in a way that does you any kind of justice? Even if I knew every name in the world and gathered them all together like so many precious garlands of flowers, I still could not give you an adequate name. Is it better to remain still and silent before you?

All I can say is that you are Love beyond all my understanding. And all I want to ask is that your kingdom may come in me and in us. Amen.

Patience

When Jesus speaks about the kingdom in the Gospels, he is introducing a genuine revolution. He is proposing a new kind of life where God is Lord, liberating us from evil and giving us lasting freedom. The parables of Jesus urge us to repent and also promise us mercy: both themes are marvellously intertwined in the parable of the prodigal son, which could also be called the parable of the merciful father (Lk 15:11–32). The miracles of Jesus are compelling signs of the kingdom: he heals people to show that the kingdom is already present; he casts out spirits to demonstrate that no evil can withstand its loving dominion.

Since this book is about a mindful approach to the Lord's Prayer, it makes sense to reflect on the unhurried growth of the kingdom, and how we are invited to mirror its calm development by exercising the virtue of patience. The kingdom of God is a divine enterprise, and like all divine actions, it is characterised by measured yet definite progress. God is patient, and God knows how to wait.

In the fourth chapter of Mark's Gospel, Jesus compares the kingdom of God to a man who scatters seed on the ground. He sleeps and rises, and each day he notices that the seed has sprouted and grown, but he doesn't know how. The kingdom is like this: it begins unobtrusively like small seeds, yet is unstoppable in power, blossoming into life in all its fullness. In the same chapter, Jesus compares the kingdom of God to a mustard seed sown in the ground that springs up and grows into a large plant, offering shelter to the birds of the air. Seeds do not become plants overnight; the process takes time. These parables about the kingdom suggest that patience is vital.

The person with whom you must first exercise patience is yourself. Easier said than done. 'I want perfection and I want it now', as someone once said. Becoming a perfect Christian isn't a matter of pulling a rabbit out of a hat. However eager you are to see your cup spilling over with goodness, the cup needs to be filled first. Tradition has it that Jesus fell three times as he carried the cross up the hill of Calvary; and each time he got up again. You need to be patient with a similar rhythm of falling and rising as you ascend the mountain of love. Your progress won't be as smooth or as fast as you might like.

The good news is that God doesn't demand of you the immediate perfection that you demand of yourself. God rejoices in your efforts; he is not fixated on results. God values the energy you put into achieving results, whether or not you get the actual results. And the events that seem to block your progress may in fact help it: you want to escape from a talkative person in order to pray whereas that person may actually be God's way of giving you the opportunity to grow in patience. If you willingly 'waste' time with a person who irritates you, God will help you make up for lost time later.

Jesus exercised extraordinary patience. He didn't suddenly materialise on earth as a fully-fledged adult. Instead, he submitted himself to a lengthy process of growth and preparation. This began with nine months in Mary's womb. After that, there were thirty years before his public ministry actually began. Even professions with the longest schooling – surgery or psychiatry – only require about a third of the time that Jesus spent in quiet preparation for his ministry.

Once his three years of public life began, this pattern of patience continued. Over and over again Jesus demonstrated exceptional patience, putting up with apostles who couldn't understand him, with Pharisees who refused to understand him, with people who initially understood him but then chose to misunderstand him, and ultimately with people who denied him, betrayed him, abandoned him and crucified him.

Lord Jesus, you spent nine months in Mary's womb; you spent decades living quietly in Nazareth. But I'm in a hurry to go forward. I always want to move on quickly. I want so many new experiences that I don't take time to savour what is before me. Give me the patience to change my schedule so that I follow your timing and not my own.

Desiring the Kingdom

A mother is in a supermarket. Her young son is with her. It's the end of the afternoon. She has purchased all her groceries. They stand in line before the checkout. The last thing she wants is for her little boy to eat a bar of chocolate before they go home for dinner. He knows what his mother thinks, but he thinks differently. He tugs at his mother's coat, pleads over and over again, and finally he looks up at her with such a beseeching look that she simply cannot turn down his request.

That boy who begs his mother for chocolate is an example of prayer in action: prayer in its root meaning of asking earnestly or pleading. Of course, the boy is not asking something earnestly of God, but pleading with his mother. Prayer expresses our desires. If prayer doesn't express our desires, our prayer is of no use. If you don't have any desire for something, why would you even ask for it? What we desire tells us a lot about ourselves. In the words of Anton Chekhov, 'Tell me what you want, and I'll tell you who you are.'

Desire plays an important role in every petition of the Lord's Prayer, and we could just as well have begun exploring the theme of desire while we reflected on the last petition, hallowed be thy name. In any event, desire plays an essential role in every petition, and perhaps now is as good a time as any to discuss it.

Jesus desired to free people from evil and give them life in abundance. His passion was for a new world, a kingdom of love and mercy. What kingdom do you desire? What kind of new world are you willing to spend yourself for?

If you just mumble the words 'thy kingdom come' in a mindless way, are you making a request at all? If the boy in the story above didn't want the chocolate, he wouldn't even have bothered asking his mother for it. His desire gave him the energy to make his request for the bar of chocolate and to keep asking for it. Prayer needs the wings of desire to fly; otherwise, it remains grounded and never takes off.

God values your desires and takes them seriously. God is delighted when you have generous desires. God loves responding to full-sized desires. When Jesus tells us to pray 'thy kingdom come', he wants us to seek it with real passion and desire.

Desires are powerful. They energise us, galvanise us into action and give a clear direction to our lives. So, let's desire with real passion for the kingdom of God to become a reality in our world. Good desires are really a gift from God, a grace from God. The desire for God's kingdom to come is not so much your own desire, but comes to you from the Lord. But you can help this desire of God's by seeking to nurture and deepen it in your heart.

At times you may feel ambivalent about the kingdom of God. Part of you wants it, and part of you may be quite hesitant. 'Gosh', you wonder, 'if all the world ends up loving God, what will the world be like? This may take me out of my comfort zone, into uncharted territory. Will I be able to handle it?' At the same time, it's important to try to cultivate this desire for the kingdom of God. Even if the desire is weak, pray that it might become stronger. When you pray 'thy kingdom come', you're expressing a desire, the desire that everyone in this world will come to love God and to love each other – this is what the kingdom of God means.

Again and again, we can see how central desires are in the lives of the saints. Let's take three examples.

Born in Siena in 1347, St Catherine of Siena was a laywoman and Third Order Dominican. At once a remarkable mystic and dynamic activist, she was consumed with a passion for God's glory and the salvation of souls. Catherine felt a mere nothing compared to God; yet there was something infinite in her: the unquenchable desire for God that energised her whole life. If all you want is a bar of chocolate, your desire is satisfied once you have the chocolate. If you yearn for God, your desire will never be satisfied during the course of your life, because there is no end to God. He is limitless and inexhaustible.

Catherine's desires were loving, ardent and irresistible. God rewarded her outlandish desires by making her the woman who sorted out a huge crisis within the Catholic Church in the fourteenth century. It was Catherine who persuaded the Pope to return from Avignon to Rome.

Before his conversion, St Ignatius of Loyola was ready to sacrifice his very life in order to win honour and fame in the eyes of polite society. Nothing could stop him. In 1521, he persuaded a tiny group of soldiers to defend the fortress of Pamplona against a much larger force of French soldiers. It was a crazy idea, but that didn't alarm him. He wasn't into half-measures. But once a cannonball shattered Ignatius's leg, the others gave up. Ignatius converted while he was recuperating from the battle. What attracted him to serving God was the desire to do great things as St Francis and St Dominic had done. As one of his friends said about Ignatius, God didn't choose him because he was particularly good, but because he was a man of great desires and energy, someone who never admitted defeat and never stopped fighting the good fight. God rewarded Ignatius's big desires by having him found the Jesuits. Ignatius developed a spirituality that has helped millions of people grow closer to God.

St Thérèse of Lisieux had a huge desire to be a missionary, and she had no intention of limiting her missionary activity to one country. Not only did she want to preach the Gospel on five continents; she wanted to preach on all five continents at the same time! She didn't envisage her missionary activity as lasting five years or even fifty years. In her autobiography, she wrote that she wanted to be a missionary 'from the beginning of creation until the consummation of the ages'! It was a crazy desire: to want to be a missionary everywhere at once and for the whole course of human history.

Her desire seemed to lose all its momentum once Thérèse became an enclosed Carmelite nun in Normandy, France. However, she realized that at the heart of every missionary's life is love. Thérèse read 1 Corinthians 13. It helped her see that love was at the heart of all things. She saw that if she could become love, she would be at the heart of the Church's mission. This meant that although she might be physically confined to a cloister, no cloister and no space could stop her spirit from flying to the most distant lands. God answered Thérèse's huge desire because of its intensity and strength, and this woman, who never set her foot in a missionary land and who died at the young age of twenty-four, is now patroness of the missions.

I've mentioned these three saints – Catherine of Siena, Ignatius of Loyola, and Thérèse of Lisieux – to encourage you to pray 'thy kingdom come' with huge resolve, with true passion and with genuine desire.

Lord, please plant the desire for your kingdom deep within me. And help me to make a concrete start on the way leading to your kingdom by loving you more, by being kinder toward those around me, and by cutting out the little lies and the big self-deceptions so that I can love in a truthful and genuine way.

Crazy World

As long as this world is not the kingdom of God, that is, as long as it's not a world where everyone loves God and loves each other, it will continue to be a crazy world. The kingdom of God will come: there will be a lot of blood, sweat and tears before it becomes a reality on earth. Nevertheless, its coming is sure. Despite its certain arrival, Jesus still invites you to desire it and to beseech the Father for it.

Jesus tells us to pray 'thy kingdom come', because it is so important to ask God that every man, woman and child will come to know and love him. When you're asking for God's kingdom to come, you're asking for this world to be transformed into a world of love and compassion. That's why the final chapter of the final book of the Bible culminates in this heartfelt cry, one of the most beautiful – and shortest – prayers ever composed by a human being: 'Come, Lord Jesus' (Rev 22:20).

Whenever you see problems in this world, don't allow yourself to be dragged down. Turn instead to God and make your desires stronger than ever, begging him with all your heart: 'Lord, may your kingdom come. May your kingdom come everywhere. May every human being turn to you, may every human being learn to love and serve you'. It sounds like an impossible dream, but I challenge you to dream it.

Jesus tells us, 'Seek the kingdom of God and his justice, and all the rest will be given you as well' (Lk 12:31). So, Jesus is saying: don't get too concerned about money, about honour, about prestige or even about your health. He's saying: you focus on God's needs, and God will take care of you.

The Father guides everything, so don't be so stubborn as to want to do it all by yourself. Just turn trustingly to God for help. A marvellous exchange – you concern yourself with God's interests, and God will take care of your needs. We will be much happier people, and our world will lose its craziness, if we put God's agenda, God's interests and God's kingdom first.

In the Gospel of Matthew, Jesus says something rather surprising, 'the kingdom of heaven has suffered violence, and violent people take it by force' (Mt 11:12). It seems a strange statement. After all, we don't want more violence. We already have too much violence in this mad world of ours (to use the title of that song by Tears for Fears). The kind of violence that Jesus is talking about here is the violence you need to exercise against your evil impulses. It is the violence involved in making difficult sacrifices, in putting others first. It is the violence involved in accepting the difficult days as well as the good days. It is the violence of uniting all these little sacrifices of yours with the enormous sacrifice Jesus has made by laying down his life for you. If you have a strong desire to see God's kingdom come, this desire will give you the strength to struggle against your own egoism. It will take you beyond self-concern, so that you live more and more for others.

St Paul reminds us that we do not simply stroll into heaven in an absent-minded manner. He tells us, 'I have fought the good fight; I have finished the race; I have kept the faith' (2 Tim 4:7).

While you can trust in God's infinite mercy, you also need to do something, realizing of course that it is not your own efforts that ultimately count: it is with the Father's help and through the infinite merits of his Son Jesus Christ that you will receive the reward God so wants to give you.

Lord, when I see bad things going on in this world, help me not to lose hope. Don't let these bad things stop me from dreaming the impossible dream of 'thy kingdom come'. Remind me at moments like that to cry out to you with huge desire, enormous trust and great confidence: 'Lord, may your kingdom come. May every human being turn to you, may every human being learn to love you and to serve you.'

The Kingdom of God Makes Us Royal

The truth is that each one of us is a monarch. It is not just the prerogative of royal families. Because of the kingdom of God, we have all been granted a royal identity. We need to surprise ourselves and others with words such as 'prince' and 'princess' that connect us to our greatest hopes and desires. We need words that open us up to the unvisited layers of our own humanity. We need to give less 'airtime' to words that trivialise our lives, that shrink our very selves.

Who is deciding your identity for you? Take the example of the radio. Whenever I listen to the radio, I hear myself and other Irish people described as taxpayers, workers, students, commuters, citizens, consumers, native-born or immigrants, healthy, sick, young, old, sports fans, music lovers, married, single, homeowners, drivers, pedestrians, cyclists, filmgoers … I never recall myself or fellow Irishmen and Irishwomen being described on mainstream radio as children of God or as immortal (apart from the limited context of occasional niche programmes such as broadcasted radio Masses). We rarely hear words in public discourse that do justice to our true depth, the kinds of words I find in the best-selling Irish writer of all time, who by the way is not James Joyce or Maeve Binchy but C.S. Lewis.

This Belfast-born writer who died the same day that John F. Kennedy was assassinated (22 November 1963) gave a magnificent sermon in the Church of Saint Mary the Virgin, Oxford on 8 June 1941. In the darkness of the Second World War, he introduced a shaft of light through speaking in a majestic manner about the wonder of being truly human. His sermon was called 'The Weight of Glory'. Allow me to cite just two extracts.

There are no *ordinary* people. You have never talked to a mere mortal. Nations, cultures, arts, civilization – these are mortal, and their life is to ours as the life of a gnat. But it is immortals whom we joke with, work with, marry, snub, and exploit – immortal horrors or everlasting splendours.

It is a serious thing to live in a society of possible gods and goddesses, to remember that the dullest and most uninteresting person you may talk to may one day be a creature which, if you saw it now, you would be strongly tempted to worship, or else a horror and corruption such as you now meet, if at all, only in a nightmare. All day long we are, in some degree, helping each other to one or other of these destinations. It is in the light of these overwhelming possibilities, it is with the awe and the circumspection proper to them, that we should conduct all our dealings with one another, all friendships, all loves, all play, all politics.

Graced Words

How can we change the way we look at ourselves? We need to become aware of how loaded our words really are. Our words carry a whole worldview, and like an iceberg, most of it is under the surface, because there are all sorts of hidden images and assumptions underlying the words we actually use. These images and assumptions shape our feelings, our attitudes, and our actions, which in turn shape our habits, our characters and even our destinies. Sure, there is the conscious level where we are aware of our words, but there is also the level where there is so much that we don't see and recognise but which still affects us profoundly.

Our words, and the images and metaphors they contain, are shaping how we see things and the way we live. We have absorbed these words, and we take them for granted, but we need to start putting them into question. Words are both creative and destructive, because words are both the problem and the solution, words are where we are wounded, but they are also the way to healing. Words can and do limit us, but words can also lift us up to bigger hopes and more generous possibilities.

Words are so creative that in the first chapter of Genesis God speaks and the world comes into being. Now, that's power! From the dawn of creation, God has communicated with us through words. *The* Word of all words is the Word of God: 'in the beginning was the Word, and the Word was with God, and the Word was God' (Jn 1:1). The Prologue of John's Gospel goes on to tell us, 'Through him all things were made' (Jn 1:3). It is through the creative Word of God that the world comes into being. As the Letter to the Hebrews tells us: 'God ... has spoken to us through the Son ... through whom also he created the world' (Heb 1:1–2).

Jesus is not simply *a* Word of God. Everything was created not through any words, but through *the* Word, the *Logos*, who is the Son, and in the Spirit who is Love. Jesus Christ is the Word of God: this is a clear sign of how important words are. Words are creative because of *the* Word.

We need to learn to talk as though it were for the first time – all over again. Jesus came to save us. A vital part of being saved is that our words need to be redeemed – just as much as the rest of us. We need divine help to change our way of speaking and the content of what we say. We need to ask the Word who is God to transform our human words into healing words. Graced words, inspired by *the* Word who is God, can help us to see the world in a new way.

I'd like to propose three creative 'languages' corresponding to the three tenses of every human life: the past, the present and the future. We could call these three languages the Emmaus language, the Evangelical language, and the Easter language.

The Emmaus language teaches us to look at our past in a positive way, to discover seeds of peace where we once only found grounds for fear. In the story from the Gospel of Luke that unfolds on the road to Emmaus, the two disciples first share with an unknown stranger (who is in fact Jesus) the disappointment that weighs upon them, and he then helps them to reframe their past in a new light. Jesus does not force them to ignore their wounds but patiently listens to their struggles. This story of the disciples on the road demonstrates that the Emmaus language is not about the magic of instantaneous transformation. We must go through a healing process. We must first unburden ourselves of the wounds of the past, before we can arrive at speaking about our past with graced words.

The Evangelical language helps us to live in a new way in the 'now'. As you know, the word 'evangelical' comes from the Greek word '*evangelion*', which means good (*eu*) message (*angelion*). It helps us describe others as they really are: the children of God, true royalty. If we can make the leap of faith that enables us to see God in our neighbours, and in the events unfolding in our lives, we will find it much easier to speak words of 'good news' to them.

The third language, the Easter language, helps us hope that despite signs of decay and death, our ultimate future is life in all its abundance. The Easter language invites us not to be afraid, because God whispers words of loving hope in our hearts. The future belongs to God, and nothing can come between us and God's love in Christ Jesus Our Lord. And so, as we face the future, the Easter language teaches us to speak words that are bold and daring.

Renewing our ways of speaking about the three tenses of our lives will enable us to discern new openings in our past, our present and our future. By ourselves, we cannot learn this liberating language, but if we allow ourselves to be graced by 'God-words', our hearts will burn within us.

Father, the gift of speech is the most useful gift you have given us. With it, we can turn to you in praise and thanksgiving. We can make you known and loved to those around us. We can reassure them, raise their spirits, and express our affection for them. Give us the grace to speak in creative and upbuilding ways. Help us to recognise that we are surrounded by brothers and sisters who are princes and princesses. May our human words echo those of your Son, the sublime and self-giving Divine Word. Amen.

Chapter Five

Thy Will Be Done

When your will is God's will, you will have your will.
Charles Spurgeon

The Wisdom of Surrender

The earth orbits around the sun and the little acorn grows into an enormous oak tree. To express these realities differently, the earth and the acorn are obeying God's will. God has a plan and design for the planet and for the acorn, and they follow God's plan. And in following God's plan, they blossom and thrive – and so do we. God takes care of these and of many other amazing processes of movement and growth that are constantly happening in this enormous universe of ours.

Imagine the earth were to say, 'I'm fed up of orbiting the sun at this speed; I want to take things easy for a while'. If the earth slowed down the speed of its orbit, it would actually fly straight toward the sun, and we'd all be dead, long before the earth actually plunged into the sun.

Imagine if all the seeds of the world were to say, 'We've no intention of becoming trees, because it's much more fun remaining as we are'. If there were no trees, we would all die, because trees produce most of the oxygen that we breathe.

If the earth, the seeds and other parts of nature were to make up their own laws, we'd have chaos, disaster and destruction. But we human beings have the gift of free will. We can decide whether to surrender to God's plan or not.

Nature doesn't act on a whim; it follows God's plan. Though here as an aside, and an extraordinarily important one at that, it must be said that we human beings are interfering with God's plan for nature. We are upsetting the cosmic laws. More and more we are witnessing the tragic results – reversals of seasons with prolonged heat in winter, bursts of severe cold in summer, torrential rains in the dry season and drought when there should be rain. Plants and trees are deceived by these changes, starting to blossom and bear fruit at the wrong times, and are therefore no longer strong enough to do so when the time is right.

In this context, Benedict XVI uttered remarkably prescient words at the beginning of his pontificate, 24 April 2005, 'there are so many kinds of desert. There is the desert of poverty, the desert of hunger and thirst, the desert of abandonment, of loneliness, of destroyed love. There is the desert of God's darkness, the emptiness of souls no longer aware of their dignity or the goal of human life. The external deserts in the world are growing, because the internal deserts have become so vast. Therefore, the earth's treasures no longer serve to build God's garden for all to live in, but they have been made to serve the powers of exploitation and destruction.'

If we pay attention to simple things like flowers and bees, we will learn about something huge from these tiny things. We will learn about infinity and eternity, because the will of God finds gracious expression in minute atoms as much as in gigantic galaxies.

Father, teach me to see your love in the feel of a grain of sand, in the song of a robin, and in the sight of the rising sun. Help me to believe that life is not a chance series of events, but a miraculous unfolding guided by your hand. May my life itself become a song of praise to you.

Bloom Where You're Planted

Each football player in a team does not need to know the overall strategy of the team. As long as all players do what they are asked to do, the strategy will work according to plan. If every player were to follow his own plan, mass confusion would result. A badly coordinated plan has never helped a football team to win a match.

One major obstacle to doing God's will is our refusal to bloom where we're planted. We don't want to be where we find ourselves and we don't want to do what we are supposed to be doing.

What does it mean to do God's will? First, it means observing the Ten Commandments. Second, it means that in the situation in which you find yourself – whether that be family life, single life,

life as a religious, a priest, or whatever – you love God with all your heart and strength, and you love your neighbour as yourself. Sometimes, almost without realising it, you can try to escape the state of life in which you find yourself.

As a little child, St Thérèse of Lisieux read the story of St Joan of Arc, this girl from a poor family, who despite no military training, had such charisma that she led the French army to a momentous victory over the English in the city of Orléans. As a result of reading the life of Joan of Arc, Thérèse felt that she too was called to do great things. But at the time, she equated great things with spectacular exploits. Later she realised that in order to become a saint, eye-catching melodrama was not necessary. Thérèse realised that she could become a saint in a more hidden way.

Each state of life has its specific duties. For instance, a wife has duties to her husband and children. God would never call her to abandon these duties by giving all her energy to charitable work in her local parish. At the same time, God would never call a parish priest to neglect his service to his parishioners. Sometimes the priest himself feels that if only he has less to do, he can give more time to prayer and contemplation. The great French saint, the Curé of Ars, who is the patron saint of parish priests, was several times tempted to leave his own parish and withdraw to a place where he could give more time to prayer. Luckily for his parishioners and for countless others who sought his help, the Curé's monastic dreams were always thwarted.

Let's say a good Christian father who is an introvert has four lively, noisy children. Now, given the fact that introverts need time on their own, he will naturally find it difficult to be around the children all the time. That's fine; he needs time on his own. But he might find himself increasingly drawn to extended periods of quiet prayer and lengthy spiritual reading. He won't necessarily realise that by getting more and more absorbed by these times of quiet, he is neglecting his children.

In devoting ourselves to the duties of our state of life, it's difficult to find the right balance. There is no hard-and-fast rule; there is no single rule of thumb that works in every situation and for all times.

At certain times a husband will find he needs to give a lot of time to his wife and children; at other times, he may need to stop and give more time to prayer. The circumstances of our lives change, so do our own energies, and so do the needs of those who rely on us.

Father, I want your will to be done in my life. But I'm not always sure what my priorities should be and how to keep everything balanced. Help me to give priority to what is central, and not get side-tracked by things that are less important. Help me to find the right balance between work and rest, so that I won't just be busy, but will bear fruit.

I Did It Whose Way?

Ultimately, there are only two ways of living: my way or God's way. One day St Thérèse of Lisieux was working in the laundry. The nun opposite her was washing handkerchiefs. The good sister kept splashing Thérèse with dirty water. Thérèse wanted to pull back and theatrically wipe her face to show the sister it would be better if she calmed down. After all, a fellow sister splashing water all over her wasn't something that corresponded with her dream of religious life.

In a way, it is not that hard to do great things. If someone is drowning, we are likely to jump into the water to save them. In a dramatic situation such as this, it is easy to get carried away by the greatness of what we're doing. If our country goes to war, we may volunteer to enter the army. The admiration of our fellow citizens sweeps us along so that we feel energised and up for it. We like performing magnificent feats and dazzling exploits, and often we begin to think really highly of ourselves as a result.

To put up with the little idiosyncrasies and foibles of the people we have to live with – that is a different matter! In part because we ourselves haven't chosen to put up with these people; putting up with them isn't our *will*. We're stuck with someone whom we never wanted to be with in the first place.

St Thérèse decided to welcome being splashed with dirty water as a gift from God, and so she resolved not to show any signs of annoyance to her fellow sister. By enduring this discomfort, she knew she was pleasing God and doing his will more fruitfully than if she had followed her own will and set off to be martyred in a foreign land.

In fact, Thérèse found many opportunities in her convent to do things God's way rather than her way. She was really put out by the way one of her fellow sisters always rattled her beads when the community came together in the chapel to pray. Thérèse could have stopped this by sending a long withering glance in the direction of this sister. Instead, she welcomed with gratitude this opportunity to renounce her own will. She saw this as God's gift, irritating for her ego certainly, but still a gift.

The funny thing is that the person in your life whom you feel the deepest antipathy toward could be the very person who will make you holy. The person to help you be holy probably won't be the person you find easiest to love, because as Jesus says in the Gospel of Luke, 'If you love those who love you, what credit is that to you? For even sinners love those who love them' (Lk 6:32).

As St Thérèse endured her final illness, she received wonderful care from her fellow sisters. Moreover, she was no longer able to work in the laundry, so that sister was no longer splashing the dirty water all over her; she was no longer able to go to choir, so she no longer had the irritation of the sister rattling her beads. Now she had new enemies: she was tormented by the buzzing flies in her room that also landed on her sick body. But since God told her to forgive her enemies, it struck her that these flies presented her with an ideal opportunity to practice this forgiveness. Thérèse realised that extravagant penances would have tempted her to glorify herself and say, 'Look how great I am!' But these little annoyances didn't give her any glory. They also made her turn to God for help: repeatedly she came face to face with her own limitations, the limits of her patience and good will, and she had to ask God to rescue her.

Lord, I thank you for my life as it is. I thank you especially for all the people who annoy me. I thank you for the people who irritate me so much that I realise how little patience I really have.

Holy in God's Way

If I've mentioned St Thérèse of Lisieux so often, it's because there are so many stories from her short life that help us understand concretely what it means to do God's will. When it comes to the will of God, we can find ourselves thinking, 'Gosh, if only I didn't have to deal with such and such a difficult person in my life, I could really get on with the task of being holy'. This lament is in effect a way of saying – my will be done. I want to be holy according to my vision of how holiness should unfold. And in my vision of holiness, this particularly difficult person shouldn't enter into the picture at all. They're ruining the beautiful tapestry I've weaved together in my mind. St Thérèse realised that it's God's will that I become holy precisely through these people whom I find so irritating. People who infuriate me are not a barrier to holiness; on the contrary, they are actually the gate through which I must enter into the holiness that God wants for me.

There was one nun in the convent who totally exasperated Thérèse. Everything about this sister – the way she spoke, the way she moved, her temperament and character – seemed expressly designed to drive Thérèse to distraction. But Thérèse never expressed the slightest sign of displeasure; she never gave vent to her anger. While recognising her annoyance, she tried to deal with it as best she could. Sometimes Thérèse found this nun's presence simply unbearable; at those moments she would descend the back stairs of the convent simply to avoid her. But most of the time Thérèse just got on with life and decided not to give in to her own sense of irritation. Each time she found herself with this difficult nun, Thérèse grasped this as an opportunity to embrace God's will.

As a result, this difficult nun became Thérèse's threshold to a new way of living. Thanks to this nun who aggravated her so intensely, Thérèse moved beyond impatience to patience, beyond anger to gentleness and beyond irritation to kindness. To this most unlikely of sources, Thérèse owed three sublime fruits of the Holy Spirit – patience, gentleness and kindness.

Let's say there is a really difficult colleague in your workplace. One day you breathe a huge sigh of relief: news comes through that this troublesome person is being transferred to a different branch of the company in another part of town. All of a sudden you have a smile on your face. Nothing can dampen your spirits as you join in the going-away party. On this person's last day in the office, you watch them clear out their desk. They say goodbye, and you wish them every success. You wait until they are safely out of the building and you throw your arms up in the air – whoopee! What happens next? This difficult person is replaced by a new person who is even worse!

Thy will be done! It isn't easy!

Lord, there are difficult people in my life, and I'm often at a loss as to how to deal with them. Since you are Lord of my life, there must be a reason that these people are still around. I thank you for their presence, even and especially when they annoy me. They show me how poor and limited I am, and how much I need your help, and that is already something for which to be grateful. Thank you for these people.

Messengers of God's Will

In the Gospel of Luke, the angel Gabriel invites the Virgin Mary to become the mother of Jesus, the mother of God. And Mary replies, 'Here am I, the servant of the Lord; let it be with me according to your word' (Lk 1:38).

Each of us has an angel at our side: 'the angel of the Lord encamps around those who fear him and delivers them' (Ps 34:7). This angel watches over our every step: 'For he will command his angels concerning you to guard you in all your ways' (Ps 91:11).

Your angel speaks to you in many ways. Through a member of your family or a good friend, or even through the words of someone you've only met for the first time. Through a phrase that particularly strikes you when you are reading a book or an article, a phrase that urges you toward greater love. When you contemplate a spectacular sunset or gaze in wonder at the stars lighting up the night sky, your angel gives you a sense of how great God is and of how small everything else is compared to God. The unheard voice of your angel speaks to you in so many situations, always encouraging you to do good and avoid evil.

The Virgin Mary shows us how to respond to the voice of our Angel. 'Here am I, the servant of the Lord; let it be with me according to your word.'

It's important not to give this response in a mechanical way. You need to put life, feeling and love into it: 'Yes, I am happily your servant Lord, and whatever you want of me, I give my full yes to it.'

A reply such as this gives you the strength to accept what God is asking of you. When you acquire the habit of saying yes to God in all the little and big events of life, the Word becomes flesh within you. God comes to live in your heart, God acts in your life, and God flows out from you to others.

Lord, help me to be alert and attentive to the voice of the angel at my side, because this angel speaks your words to me. Each evening as I look back at the events of the day, give me light to see the moments when your angel has been speaking words of encouragement and life. Help me to reply with Mary: 'Here am I, the servant of the Lord; let it be with me according to your word.'

Becoming More than I Am

Our energy and time are taken up by many things that neither count nor last. We run around in circles chasing what doesn't really matter. As one of the psalms puts it: 'how long will your hearts be closed, how long will you love what is futile and seek what is false?' (Ps 4:3). Jesus tells us clearly that the most important thing of all is to 'love the Lord your God with all your heart and with all your soul and with all your mind and with all your strength' (Mk 12:30). This is the meaning of doing the will of God, the will of the Father of Jesus, who is also 'Our Father'.

Even more than doing the will of God, and to do God's will is already to do something stupendous, you can fulfil it in an even deeper way by placing yourself completely in Jesus, so that all you do is done in him. In that case, not only do you *do* the will of God, you *are* in the will of God. 'Abide in me, and I in you' (Jn 15:4). St Elizabeth of the Trinity says that we must be transformed into Jesus Christ. Certainly, God loves me as I am; but at the same time God loves me too much to want me stay *as* I am.

The incarnation happened two thousand years ago when Jesus was born of the Virgin Mary. God doesn't want the incarnation to stop there. Jesus was never a nurse, but he becomes one through every nurse who decides to live her or his demanding call as Jesus would have lived it. Jesus was never the mother of a family, but he becomes one through every mother who decides to devote herself to her husband and children as Jesus would have done. Jesus was never a priest in the twenty-first century, but he becomes one through every priest who lives his calling with Jesus' own generosity and love. Jesus wants to be incarnated once again in you and me, so that each of us can say as St Paul once said: 'it is no longer I who live, but it is Christ who lives in me' (Gal 2:20).

This means, as St John the Baptist said, that 'He must increase, but I must decrease' (Jn 3:30). Your personality won't be destroyed in the process. Paradoxically, you'll become more yourself thanks to this mysterious transformation. What you will shed are the stubborn layers of ego and of selfishness. As Jesus says in the Gospel of John: the Father 'removes every branch in me that bears no fruit. Every branch that bears fruit he prunes to make it bear even more fruit' (Jn 15:2).

If you fear becoming more like Christ, if you feel it's only a recipe for sorrow, you can benefit from Mary's help. She gave a full and generous yes to God. She knows that God wants your happiness. She is also honest and doesn't deny that there will be pain. At the same time, she will reassure you that you can be happy even during the painful moments, just like someone who happily undergoes a costly sacrifice for a close friend. She encourages you, showing you that challenging moments give you the opportunity to show God how much you love him.

O Virgin Mary, help me in the small and big challenges of life, so that I can belong to those who do everything in God and for God. Amen.

As in Heaven

Karl Rahner, the German Jesuit and theologian, once remarked that the Christian of the twenty-first century would either be a mystic or else wouldn't be a Christian at all, but what kind of mystic? As climate change affects us more and more, we're becoming increasingly aware that any worthwhile mysticism needs to seek God in all things, especially in our relationship with the rest of creation.

Unless our mysticism inspires us to care for our common home, we won't have a common home, and we ourselves shall vanish from the face of the earth.

How can we become more mystical in this new millennium? By doing God's will on earth as it is done in heaven. What does this mean? It's not a matter of praying louder and longer or of going to church as often as we can. The danger of an overdose of piety is that we become preoccupied with *ourselves* and with *our* holiness. And then if someone prevents us from saying our prayers or getting to church, we become angry and our so-called holiness suddenly disappears. Woe betide anyone who has the temerity to stand between us and our will!

We can become too attached even to our own sinfulness so that we never learn to trust God's forgiveness. As far as the east is from the west, so far does God remove our transgressions from us, as Psalm 103 tells us. God's forgiveness is always bigger than any wrong we do. We often find it difficult to trust that God could be loving enough to forgive us. Perhaps God is even more wounded by this lack of trust than by our sins.

Doing God's will on earth as it is done in heaven – this sounds like a tall order, so tall that it appears completely out of reach. How could we possibly carry out God's will as the blessed saints do in heaven? The reason this noble enterprise seems preposterous is because we tend to base holiness on our own merits. As children we were taught that if we behaved properly, we would be rewarded. 'Do your homework and then you can go out and play. But if you don't do your homework, you must stay inside.' We were taught that we had to earn love. If we did the right thing, our parents and teachers would love us in return. We transpose this kind of behaviour to God himself. We reason that the heavenly Father acts exactly like those whose love we had to earn. We figure that we must do our utmost and put on our best performance to have any hope of deserving God's love and acceptance.

God, however, doesn't follow human logic: as high as the heavens are above the earth, so high are God's ways above our ways. God doesn't ask us to earn his love; instead, God asks us to receive his love! When we finally learn to take in God's love, we shall no longer even want to sin, because we shall no longer want to go elsewhere to find what we have already found so abundantly in God, 'Lord, to whom can we go? You have the words of eternal life' (Jn 6:68).

The more we entrust ourselves to the adventure of love, the more our fears will diminish, until one day they will evaporate altogether. Perfect love casts out fear. God is a fire of love. He is eternal love. His love never ceases. Our fears surface easily and often: we remember the bad things we've done, and we ask ourselves how God could still possibly love us. We find it so difficult to focus our hearts and minds on God's love for us; we focus on ourselves and our shortcomings, often with sad and even tragic consequences.

It's only possible to do God's will on earth as it's done in heaven through a free, gratuitous gift of God. And God is only too ready to give us this kind of gift, a gift we don't need to earn or merit. The choice is ours: do we want to stay trapped in our human will, with its hang-ups, its compulsion to impress people, to perform and to be liked, its resentments and fears? Or are we ready to take the risk of total confidence in God, trusting that this confidence will disarm him so much that he will turn a blind eye to our shortcomings and faults?

We don't trust God enough to believe he could possibly make saints of us. We cannot picture ourselves as members of such an elite club. Yet, as Pope Francis has argued so clearly and persuasively in *Gaudete et Exsultate*, sanctity is not for the privileged few. It is a gift offered to everyone, including you and me. Pope Francis uses everyday examples to show how holiness grows through many small steps:

This holiness to which the Lord calls you will grow through small gestures. Here is an example: a woman goes shopping, she meets a neighbour and they begin to speak, and the gossip starts. But she says in her heart: 'No, I will not speak badly of anyone'. This is a step forward in holiness. Later, at home, one of her children wants to talk to her about his hopes and dreams, and even though she is tired, she sits down and listens with patience and love. That is another sacrifice that brings holiness. Later she experiences some anxiety, but recalling the love of the Virgin Mary, she takes her rosary and prays with faith. Yet another path of holiness. Later still, she goes out onto the street, encounters a poor person and stops to say a kind word to him. One more step. (*Gaudete et Exsultate*, 16)

Father, I'd like to believe I could be holy, but I'm a broken person in a broken world. My only hope is in Jesus. He made the dumb speak, the blind see, and the deaf hear. Open my eyes, my ears, my mouth. Give me the power to keep believing that holiness is also possible for me, especially when my strength leaves me and all I can feel is my weakness. Your generosity is beyond anything I can imagine: please make me more and more like Jesus.

CHAPTER SIX

Our Daily Bread

The bread which you do not use is the bread of the hungry;
the garment hanging in your wardrobe is the garment of
him who is naked; the shoes that you do not wear are the shoes
of the one who is barefoot; the money that you keep locked away
is the money of the poor; the acts of charity that you do not
perform are so many injustices that you commit.
St Basil the Great

Up until this point in the prayer that Jesus taught his disciples, everything has been directed toward the Father himself. Before asking anything for ourselves, we raised our minds and hearts up to heaven and committed ourselves to his name, his kingdom and his will. The first part of the prayer was directed God-wards. In the second part of the prayer, the direction changes. Having asked for God's name to be kept holy, his kingdom to come and his will to be done, the focus is now on our needs.

Give Us Our Bread

It's surely no accident that this petition contains both the words 'us' and 'our'. By using two 'we' words, Jesus is reinforcing the importance of going beyond our individual needs. Whenever I ask God for what I need, I should never ask only for myself. Neither should I ask only for my own family, my own relatives or my own friends. I should include all those in need of bread of whatever kind.

Daily bread is not only intended for me or my small group but for all of us. That is why the Father rejoices when we gather money and provisions to help those in distant lands who suffer from hunger. Since everyone is a child of God, the Father is delighted to see his children reaching out to help each other. At times we worry that the money we raise will not arrive at its destination and will not help those who really deserve it. God looks at the spirit in which we perform our actions rather than at the results of these actions. The Father simply wants us to give from a generous heart.

Although we worry that we might not be giving our surplus bread or financial aid to those who deserve it, we don't ask if we ourselves deserve all that we already have. It doesn't strike us that having an abundance of material things provides us with the opportunity to share what we have with others. What happens instead is that the more we have, the more we want. The more we possess, the more we tend to compare ourselves with others who have even more than ourselves. We don't readily spare a thought for those who have much less.

An interesting article appeared in *The Atlantic* in 2018 about why so many super-rich people are unhappy. Written by Joe Pinsker, it was called 'The Reason Many Ultrarich People Aren't Satisfied with Their Wealth'. Pinsker found that many big millionaires and billionaires have so much money that it is actually difficult for them to spend it, even if they splash out on expensive items and luxury goods. When they reach a certain level of wealth another million dollars has a negligible impact on their already lavish lifestyle. Pinsker referred to Michael Norton, a professor at Harvard Business School, who maintains that the super-rich ask themselves two key questions to decide if they are happy: am I doing better than I did before? Am I doing better than everyone else? In order to answer these two questions, they look for things they can measure easily. Some important qualities are difficult to measure, goodness and love, for example. Money is easy to quantify, so it is a favoured measure of the super-rich. Using money as a yardstick, they can immediately determine if they're doing better than before and better than others: they simply look at the size of their house, the number of houses they have, the price of their cars, the number of cars they possess and whether they now have more than before, and if they possess more than others.

A couple with a luxury home in a middle-class neighbourhood may be wealthier than all their neighbours, but if they move to an upper-class neighbourhood, they will no longer feel as secure in their wealth. The relationship between wealth and fulfilment can easily shift. Extremely wealthy people often suffer from perpetual insecurity, because there is no fixed amount of wealth that guarantees happiness. Norton surveyed a significant number of rich people regarding what they needed to be happy. Irrespective of whether they were minor millionaires or comfortable billionaires, practically everyone said they would need two or three times their current wealth in order to guarantee happiness. Their real worry was not whether they had enough money to buy a private jet, but whether they had as much or more than other wealthy people with whom they were comparing themselves. Their focus was not so much on possessions themselves, but on what they needed in order to keep up with others and maintain their status.

If we already have much more daily bread than we actually need, how can we genuinely pray this petition in the Our Father? Perhaps by seeing ourselves as the means by which God gives others their daily bread. Our abundance can enable others to satisfy their hunger. We have received more so that those who have less may receive enough. Although God could give direct help to those in need, he values our generosity to others so highly that he does not want to deprive us of the possibility of exercising it.

Even if we're not ultra-rich, it's easy to fall prey to a sense of sadness at the possessions of others, together with a desire to have these same possessions ourselves. Envy causes such sadness at the wealth of others that this poison drains our happiness and destroys our joy. There is an antidote: gratitude. A sense of thankfulness dissolves the poison of envy. When we're envious, we focus resentfully on another person's blessings. When we're grateful, we count our own blessings. Not any kind of blessings, but important ones. Instead of becoming fixated on comparisons that in the long run are unimportant – luxury cars and mega-yachts – we pay attention to the blessings that truly count – integrity, wisdom, nobility and love. We need the sustenance of these blessings to be truly successful in life; they form an essential part of our daily bread.

Father, I thank you for delivering me from the worry of not having enough to eat. I thank you that I don't suffer from malnutrition: you really have enriched me abundantly. All too easily I pray this petition as though the phrase were – give me this day my daily bread. Help me to remember that this is a prayer for all of us. Help me to play my little part in eliminating world hunger.

Count on Him

Let's say your cousin visits you unexpectedly one evening. You offer him a cup of tea. When you're in the middle of preparing it, you realise you're out of both sugar and milk. The local store is closed. You excuse yourself for a moment, rush to your neighbour's house and say, 'I'd be really grateful if you could give me a little milk and sugar, because my cousin has just popped by, and I've practically nothing to offer him.' Your neighbour will be only too happy to help. In fact, she may even insist on giving you cake and biscuits as well.

When you pray to the Father for your daily bread, you're not just turning to a neighbour, an acquaintance or even a relatively good friend. You're turning to the best friend possible. If you're afraid that the Father won't listen to your plea for daily bread, take a few moments to remind yourself how good the Father is. The Father's goodness is beyond words and impossible to describe. That's why you can turn to him with confidence and ask him for your daily bread and for all the nourishment you need for your journey.

The Father is good to everyone. As Jesus tells us in the fifth chapter of Matthew's Gospel, the Father 'makes his sun rise on the evil and on the good and sends rain on the righteous and on the unrighteous' (Mt 5:45). In the following chapter of Matthew, Jesus invites us to reflect on the Father's goodness by looking at another part of creation: 'Look at the birds of the air: they neither sow nor reap nor gather into barns, and yet your heavenly Father feeds them. Are you not of more value than they?' (Mt 6:26) In the eleventh chapter of Luke's Gospel, Jesus asks: 'Is there anyone among you who, if your child asked for a fish, would give a snake instead of a fish? Or if the child asked for an egg, would give a scorpion? If you, then, who are evil, know how to give good gifts to your children, how much more will the heavenly Father give the Holy Spirit to those who ask him!' (Lk 11:11–13).

You need to remind yourself that the Father is the kindest, most loving and most sensitive person you could possibly imagine. As the first chapter of the Letter of St James says, every good and perfect gift comes from this Father of lights. The Father's faithfulness stretches back to time immemorial. The first chapter of the Letter to the Ephesians emphasises that the Father chose us before the foundation of the world so that we could be whole and holy before him. Not only did he choose us aeons before our birth, he also decided to 'rescue us from the power of darkness and transfer us into the kingdom of his beloved Son' (Col 1:13).

What about telling the Father how much he means to you? Here are some things you could say to him:

- When I think of you, I think of love. Thanks for being you.
- I can be myself when I'm with you.
- Each time we're together is like the first time. I'm so lucky to have you.
- You make my life complete. I feel like I've known you forever.
- I don't want to imagine my life without you.
- I want you to be my past, present and future.
- You're my last thought before going to sleep and my first thought on awakening.
- Thanks for being my reason to smile.
- I love you to the stars and back again.
- Your mercy has saved me and your wisdom keeps inspiring me.

Father, the day you walked into my life, everything changed. You mean the world to me. I want my love for you to grow stronger each moment. Thank you for yesterday, yes to today, and ... I can't wait until tomorrow.

Just for Today
If you are carrying a bucket of water, and a single drop of rain falls into it, this drop adds practically nothing to the weight you are carrying, and certainly won't throw you off balance. Scripture tells us that all the nations of the world amount to a drop of water

before God, mere dust on the scales. The weight of these nations doesn't in the least disturb his ineffable calm and equilibrium. 'Even the nations are like a drop in a bucket and are accounted as dust on the scales; see, he takes up the isles like fine dust' (Isa 40:15).

The big things in life are not always big in God's eyes. God cares more than we realise about the small stuff we're reluctant to bring to his attention: 'even the hairs of your head are all numbered' (Lk 12:7). That is why God is only too happy to answer our request for daily bread. Not only is he content with this request, more than that, he tells us only to ask for enough bread for today. We spend too much time worrying about tomorrow's bread. We miss out on the present moment because of our anxiety about the future. The worries of today are sufficient to occupy us; we can rest assured that tomorrow will take care of itself. C.S. Lewis expresses it well, 'It is only our daily bread that we are encouraged to ask for. The present is the only time in which any duty can be done or any grace received.'

'Daily bread' for 'this day' reminds us of the manna with which God fed the Israelites. After escaping from Egypt, they found themselves in the desert and began to murmur against God, blaming him for bringing them into the wilderness only to perish through starvation. In response, God started to rain down daily bread. Each morning there was a layer of dew on the ground, and when the dew evaporated in the morning sun, a delicate, white, edible substance remained.

Interestingly, a nutritional, white substance that seems to correspond to this biblical manna can still be found today throughout the Middle East. Insects that feed off the sweet sap of desert shrubs release sweet fluid secretions at night. These harden in the dry desert air and crystallise into white granules that then fall to the ground.

The Israelites used to gather manna early in the morning, since otherwise the hot sun would melt it. There is a valuable lesson hidden in this practice: we need to turn to God early in the day to ask for our daily sustenance, because otherwise our attention will be distracted by what is less wholesome, and in fact we'll suffer from spiritual malnutrition.

Manna was never meant to be hoarded. The Israelites were told to gather only enough for that day. Again, there is a helpful lesson in this command: we are not meant to cling to what nourished us in the past; we're invited to open ourselves anew to God each day.

For centuries, scholars have been tearing their hair out to discover the real meaning of the word 'daily' in 'daily bread'. This is because the Gospels of both Matthew and Luke use a particular Greek word for 'daily' in the Lord's Prayer, a word that is never otherwise used. This Greek word '*epiousios*' only appears twice – in Matthew's and Luke's version of the Lord's Prayer. It is found nowhere else in the Bible and nowhere else in all of Greek literature! On every other occasion that New Testament writers want to say 'daily', they use a common and well-known Greek word ('*hemeran*'). So why use a special word for 'daily' when it comes to the Lord's Prayer? There must be a special reason. St Jerome, the early Christian saint and scholar, hit the nail on the head by doing something quite straightforward: he translated this mysterious word in a literal way. Literally, the word '*epiousios*' means 'super-substantial'. Jerome's literal translation brings to mind the Body of Our Lord, which is higher and more exalted than any other known substance. Since this word only appears in the two Gospels, it may just have been created by Jesus and the first Christians to speak of something so special – the Eucharist – that a new term had to be coined in order to describe it.

The *Catechism of the Catholic Church* explains the full range of meanings of this rarest of Greek words much better than I could: "'Daily' (*epiousios*) occurs nowhere else in the New Testament. Taken in a temporal sense, this word is a pedagogical repetition of "this day," to confirm us in trust "without reservation." Taken in the qualitative sense, it signifies what is necessary for life, and more broadly every good thing sufficient for subsistence. Taken literally (*epi-ousios*: "super-essential"), it refers directly to the Bread of Life, the Body of Christ, the "medicine of immortality," without which we have no life within us. Finally in this connection, its heavenly meaning is evident: "this day" is the Day of the Lord, the day of the feast of the kingdom, anticipated in the Eucharist that is already the foretaste of the kingdom to come' (*CCC*, 2837).

Father, another day has begun. I'm not sure what it will bring. I'm not sure how I'll even get through this day. Your Spirit hovered over the waters on the first day of creation. May the Spirit hover over me today, and make something beautiful out of the unpromising raw material that I am.

Bread for Your Hungry Heart

In 1995 Brielle and Kyrie Jackson, twin sisters, were born twelve weeks premature. Each weighed only two pounds. At first, the two sisters were in separate incubators. One of the twins was in a critical condition. She was not expected to survive. The nurse on duty wanted to help, but how? She had a hunch that putting the twins together might just make a difference. Her hope was that the stronger girl would somehow boost the weaker one's morale. And so, against the rules of standard medical practice, the nurse put both girls into a single incubator. What happened next was nothing short of extraordinary. The stronger baby instinctively wrapped her arm around the weaker twin in a supportive embrace. Someone took a photo of that sisterly hug, and it touched millions of people around the world. As a result of that tenderest of gestures, the weaker baby's temperature stabilised, her desperate crying ceased, she started to breathe properly and her heart rate adjusted to normal. Over the following days and weeks, she grew stronger and stronger.

We all need daily bread, whether it's physical nourishment or the affection and love of others. No one – neither woman nor man – is an island. We need to inhale the air from outside to breathe. We need food to grow. We need love to thrive emotionally. We can't survive on our own.

A crying baby will often stop crying if a kind person picks it up. When they put the baby back down, it often starts crying again. Just like babies, all of us need to be held in some way. If not literally, at least in terms of being accepted and loved by others.

As well as needing the bread of physical and emotional nourishment, we also have much bigger hungers. The hunger in our hearts is deep, because our hearts are deeper than we readily acknowledge, and that hunger will never be satisfied by whatever is less than everything. The hunger of our hearts is a hunger without limits.

Like the deer that yearns for running streams, so my soul is yearning for you, my God. My soul is thirsting for God, the God of my life. When can I enter and see the face of God? By day the Lord will send his loving kindness. By night I will sing to him, praise the God of my life. (Taken from Psalm 42).

Giving Thanks

Leaving aside the miracle of the Resurrection, the only miracle found in all four Gospels is the feeding of the five thousand, where Jesus satisfies the hunger of a huge number of people with only five loaves and two fish.

The disciples of Jesus don't want the responsibility of caring for a big crowd and in a remote place to boot. They want Jesus to send these people away, so that they can find their own lodgings and their own food. In John's version, Philip exclaims that more than half a year's wages would only be enough to assure a bite of bread for everyone. Andrew adds that five loaves and two fish are of no use for so many.

Jesus isn't remotely perturbed. He takes the five loaves in his hands and give thanks. It is precisely at a moment when everything is lacking that Jesus gives thanks. In the original Greek, the word is *'eucharistesas'*, meaning 'having given thanks' (Jn 6:11). *'Eucharistesas'* – having given thanks – that's a life-changing word. The word comes from *'char'* (joy) and *'eu'* (good). It's a giving thanks that rejoices in what is good, however small and fragile the good.

This same Greek word – *'eucharistesas'* – is found in the account of the Last Supper in Luke's Gospel as well as in the account in Paul's First Letter to the Corinthians. If it were the last evening of my life, and I were facing a terrible death, would I think of giving thanks? It's more likely that I'd be a nervous wreck! If I were faced with thousands of hungry people, and all I had were five loaves and two fish, would I even take the time to be grateful? I'd probably just panic! Jesus gives thanks. That blows my mind. It's a sign of his boundless trust in the Father. If you give thanks to the Father in a terribly difficult situation, you obviously trust him enormously. All Jesus has in his hands is something radically insufficient, but the loving gratitude of Jesus opens the gateway to abundance, because his gratitude enables the Father's generosity to show itself. If you give thanks when everything around you is falling apart, that act of giving thanks helps you to hold things together, and it helps you to hold yourself together as well.

How can we find a blessing in difficult circumstances, when we feel at a total loss? By giving thanks, not some perfunctory act of thanksgiving, but an act of gratitude that truly comes from the heart. By giving thanks, we're showing that we trust that God has already blessed us in this challenging situation.

What's really important to notice is that Jesus gives thanks *before* the miracle happens. Jesus doesn't wait until after the miracle to express his gratitude. We usually postpone our acts of gratitude until we have what we want safely in our hands. That's not the way Jesus behaves. He thanks the Father first. His prayer of thanks makes a few loaves and fish multiply astoundingly.

Another important lesson to learn from this is that the first thing to do in a difficult situation is to open our eyes and see what we have before us. Jesus asks his disciples to bring him the five loaves and two fish. He gives thanks for these first blessings and for the goodness of the Father. We too should begin with the possibilities we have and then make use of them with grateful love. Complaining about what is lacking only closes down possibilities. The kind of gratitude that puts its trust in God opens up difficult situations to God's generous intervention. When we live out of this spirit of gratitude, God removes the obstacles in our path and clears the way before us.

God is always ready to help us. What's required is that we first declare before God our thankful love. This needs to be our starting point, and indeed it shouldn't only be a starting point, but a constant point of reference in our lives. As St Paul says in his First Letter to the Thessalonians: 'give thanks in every circumstance'

(1 Thess 5:18). In other words, give thanks also in difficult moments, in challenging moments, in moments when there doesn't appear to be enough resources to see you through. Beneath apparently difficult situations there is a hidden grace, and we can access that grace through our gratitude.

Our Father, you give us our daily bread, and you also give us a bread that is much more nourishing, the bread from heaven, your Son Jesus. You have made us for yourself, and our hearts are restless until they rest in you. Please guide us, draw us, and attract us toward you by the power of the Holy Spirit, so that here and now we may love you, and in the next life continue to love you forever. Amen.

The Bread of Life

In John's Gospel the people ask Jesus to do something special the day after he multiplies the loaves and fish: they want him to provide them with this kind of food each day of their lives – they want daily manna. Jesus instead offers them a much more special bread, the bread of life, 'I am the bread of life. Whoever comes to me will never go hungry, and whoever believes in me will never be thirsty' (Jn 6:35). To ask the Father for our 'daily bread' is not only to ask him for material bread or physical sustenance; it is also to ask him for the flesh of his very Son. His Son who was born in Bethlehem, a town that in the Hebrew language means 'house' (*beth*) of 'bread' (*lehem*). The Father wanted his Son to be born in the house of bread so that, like bread, he might be available to all.

The miracle of the Son giving himself as our food is so extraordinary as to be mind-boggling. It is such a powerful miracle that it leaves an indelible imprint on a person's entire life. A case in point is Pedro Arrupe, a Jesuit from the Basque country in Spain. This passionate man of God served for almost two decades as the leader of Jesuits worldwide. In 1979, before an audience of almost one-and-a-half-thousand young people gathered outside the Basilica of St Francis in Assisi, Arrupe gave a moving talk about how the Eucharist shaped his life.

Here are two of the big Eucharistic experiences that Arrupe highlighted that day. The first was a miracle he himself witnessed in Lourdes. Several weeks after his father's death, he travelled with his family to this famous Marian shrine for some spiritual peace and quiet. He was a young medical student at the time. One day while he stood in front of the large basilica with his sisters before a procession of the Blessed Sacrament began, a middle-aged woman passed by, wheeling a cart. One of Arrupe's sisters cried out, 'Look at the poor fellow in that cart!' It was the woman's twenty-year-old son, a young man badly deformed by polio. The man's mother was praying the Rosary in a loud voice, and every so often she said with a sigh, '*Maria Santissima*, help us'. He was moved to the core, and continued to watch as she hurriedly took her place in a row, awaiting the arrival of the procession. Shortly afterwards, the bishop arrived. Carrying a large host enclosed in a monstrance, he stopped to bless the young man, who gazed at the host with incredible faith. The blessing with the host was hardly finished when the young man suddenly rose to his feet, completely healed. The crowd erupted into shouts of joy.

Because Arrupe was a student of medicine, he was allowed to be present at a series of medical examinations that were subsequently carried out on the young man. The tests established that this instantaneous cure could not be explained by any natural or scientific law. As he took in this news, Arrupe thought of his professors and fellow students in the faculty of medicine back in Madrid. Many of them were atheists and some even liked to make fun of miracles. He himself could not doubt that he had witnessed a real miracle in Lourdes. This miracle made him feel that he had been standing next to Jesus, in comparison to whose power every other authority appeared insignificant. He returned to Madrid, but now he had lost all interest in the studies that previously excited him so much. His fellow students asked him, 'What's going on? You look like you're in a stupor.' In a sense, he was in another world. His mind kept returning to the miracle at Lourdes. It was fixed on that image of the host as it was raised in blessing and then of the paralyzed young man leaping from his cart. Three months later, in January 1927, Arrupe joined the Jesuits.

Another big Eucharistic experience occurred for him in the apocalyptic aftermath of the atomic bomb in Hiroshima. In 1938 Pedro Arrupe was assigned to work in Japan. He was in Hiroshima on the morning of 6 August 1945, when a nuclear weapon was detonated over the city. Although the windows of his residence were shattered, Arrupe survived, thanks to a hillock that acted as a barrier between his building and the centre of the city. He immediately started to help victims, drawing on all the skills he had acquired during more than three years of medical training.

About two weeks after the explosion, as he walked through the devastated city, Arrupe came to the spot where the house of some Christian friends had previously stood. Now there was just a makeshift hut in its place. Inside was Nakamura San, an eighteen-year-old Japanese girl whom he had baptised just a few years before. A devout Christian, she used to receive daily Communion at the 6.30am Mass celebrated each morning in the chapel of Arrupe's community.

Nakamura was lying, eyes closed, on top of a rough table a couple of feet from the ground. Her arms and legs were covered with burned rags. Her limbs looked like one big sore and continually dripped pus to the ground. Since she hadn't been able to change position for two weeks, her back was totally gangrenous, adding to the foul stench. She had only been able to eat a tiny amount of rice which her badly-injured father had managed to give her. When Arrupe tried to clean her burns, he discovered that her muscles had been reduced to pus, and this pus in turn was being eaten by a mass of worms.

Arrupe stayed by her side, at a loss for words. After a while, Nakamura opened her eyes. When she saw him next to her and smiling, two large tears formed in her eyes. She stretched out a stump of pus, where her hand had once been, and suddenly asked anxiously, 'Father, have you brought me Communion?' For two weeks, from the day the atomic bomb exploded, Nakamura had been longing for the Eucharist. Despite her horrendous suffering and her desire for an end to the pain, she desired Jesus above all, the one to whom she had given herself body and soul.

Arrupe had never before received this kind of request from someone reduced to a single, large, burning wound. Never before had anyone received the Eucharist from his hands with such desire and devotion. Not long afterwards, Nakamura breathed her last. Arrupe never forgot that girl nor the intense desire that led her to ignore her own suffering for the joy of receiving the strength and love of Jesus in the sacrament of the Eucharist.

Lord Jesus, I adore you in the obscurity of this life, where I only see through a glass, darkly. Even when I'm trying to focus on you, the light of my life, I get distracted by the shadows. But however much the twilight envelops me, I believe that you are pure goodness and mercy. One day when the shadows fall away and the dawn breaks in all its splendour, I shall see you face to face and know all you have done for me.

CHAPTER SEVEN

Forgive Us as We Forgive

When you forgive, you in no way change the past –
but you sure do change the future.
Bernard Meltzer

Receiving Forgiveness Helps Us to Forgive

An early episode in Victor Hugo's novel *Les Misérables* captures the positive effects of forgiveness in a striking way. It is an episode that will be familiar to anyone who has seen the musical *Les Mis*. Jean Valjean, a convict on parole, is hauled before a bishop from whom he has robbed a basket of silverware. The police are taken aback when the bishop makes it clear that the silverware was not stolen but a gift. In fact, the bishop insists on adding more valuables – he gives Valjean his two candlesticks as well. The bishop then requests the police to set Valjean free, since no crime was committed. Once the three gendarmes have left, the bishop explains, 'Jean Valjean, my brother, you no longer belong to evil, but to good. It is your soul that I am buying for you; I am taking it away from black thoughts and from the spirit of perdition, and I am giving it to God.'

Having been imprisoned for nineteen years for stealing a loaf of bread to feed his sister's seven starving children, Valjean's heart has become embittered at the sheer injustice of his lot. For this trifling crime, he has spent almost two decades behind bars, a prison sentence out of all proportion to his misdemeanour. Yet now, when he commits a significant theft, the bishop unexpectedly forgives him.

It is at this moment that Valjean is truly released from prison, the prison of a degraded and hardened soul. His long years behind bars have not only deprived him of freedom; they have also undermined his faith in human decency. Before we can believe we're forgiven, we need to trust in others. Trust is at the heart of forgiveness.

There are inner demons that prevent us from trusting. We need to escape these various forms of self-imprisonment. In *Les Misérables*, freedom begins to unfold through the grace Valjean receives at the hands of Bishop Myriel (whose fictional life as a pastor bears certain uncanny parallels with the real life of Jorge Mario Bergoglio, later Pope Francis).

Valjean does not undergo the magic of instantaneous transformation. Instead, a process is involved. The next episode in the novel is decisive in this respect. It is at this point that Valjean realises there is a conflict between two different selves. There is a battlefield in his heart, and he must fight against his worst self in order to become free.

The realisation dawns upon him like this: leaving the town and wandering through the open countryside, Valjean sits down behind a bush at sunset, and then hears the cheerful sound of a little boy singing as he strolls along, a hurdy-gurdy in his arm. Valjean turns around and watches as the boy tosses his handful of coins, probably his entire fortune, into the air. A coin falls to the ground and rolls toward the bush. Valjean places his foot over it. He refuses to return it to the boy, Little Gervais. When Little Gervais persists in asking for his coin, Valjean threatens him, and the child runs away sobbing.

Only then does it begin to dawn on Valjean what he has done. Overwhelmed with remorse, he searches in vain for the boy. Unable to locate him, Valjean falls to the ground, bursting into tears for the first time in nineteen years. This theft from Little Gervais has been a last-ditch attempt on the part of his savage self to regain control, but as Valjean realises the vileness of his act, something inside recoils in horror.

Valjean sees that one part of himself is intent on remaining stuck in the past, while the other part opens up a new awareness of who he is and what he can become. Will he continue to give hospitality to his familiar demons, or will he choose to walk in the light? Luckily these two contrasting courses of action do not hold equal weight. Because of the forgiveness he has received from the bishop, Valjean now feels deeply drawn by goodness. Walking in the light has become a thoroughly appealing option. The very thought of the bishop acts like a beacon that illuminates his soul. This is the light he now wants to follow, whereas the cowardly act of stealing a coin from a little child belongs to his hardened self and his brutalised past. Now this self and this past no longer hold any allure for him.

Although the effort to be forgiving will be a lifelong endeavour for Valjean, he has set free a part of himself that was blocked and buried for years, the layer of his humanity that is trusting and generous. Lewis B. Smedes, the Reformed theologian, once remarked, 'to forgive is to set a prisoner free and discover that prisoner was you'.

Father, there are so many dark zones in my heart. I've never really allowed your love to reach these cells of coldness inside. These unhappy places are where my own sulkiness and resentments continue to wound me. Can you please call on me with your gift of forgiveness? Can you please surprise and heal my wounded heart with your wonderful mercy, so that I can learn to trust and hope again?

Costly and Continual Forgiveness

In the summer of 2004, I had the privilege of meeting Steven McDonald, a New York policeman who knew what it meant to forgive. In July 1986, he and a fellow police officer stopped three teenagers who were acting suspiciously at the northern end of Central Park. Steven McDonald was talking to one of the boys, a fifteen-year-old named Shavod Jones, when the teenager suddenly pulled a gun, shooting straight at McDonald.

As he collapsed to the ground, this twenty-nine-year-old police officer saw his wife's face appear before him. At the time she was three months pregnant with their first (and what was to be their only) child. 'God, don't let me die', he prayed.

He didn't die, but he was left with injuries that changed his life forever. The first bullet entered his head above the eye. The second hit him in the throat so that he was never able to speak properly afterwards. It was the third bullet, however, that inflicted the worst damage; it shattered his spine, leaving him paralyzed from the chin down.

One of the first to visit Steven as he lay in hospital was Cardinal John O'Connor of New York. New York's senior Catholic cleric said to him, 'You feel helpless, but you remind me so much of Christ now. He didn't save the world through teaching and preaching and miracles. He made it possible when he was lying motionless on the cross. If you unite yourself and your helplessness with Christ on the cross, you are the most powerful man in the world. You'll touch people you'll never see. I can't reach out and touch them. You can.'

Steven McDonald was barely conscious at the time, but despite this he was really struck by the words, 'The most powerful man in the world'.

Six months later, while he still lay in hospital, his wife Patti Ann gave birth to their son Conor. At his son's baptism, Patti Ann read out words of forgiveness that had been written by Steven: 'I'm sometimes angry at the teenage boy who shot me. But more often, I feel sorry for him. I only hope he can turn his life into helping and not hurting people. I forgive him, and hope he can find peace and purpose in his life.'

A couple of years later, Steven McDonald sent stamps and stationery to Shavod Jones, together with a note that said, 'Let's carry on a dialogue'. He met the mother and grandmother of Shavod. Although Jones phoned him to apologise, they were never to meet after that fateful shooting. In 1995, after nine years in prison, Shavod was paroled. A few days after being released, he was the passenger on a motorbike that lost control while speeding in East Harlem. The motorbike crashed into parked cars, and Shavod died of his injuries.

Steven's son Conor absorbed the message of forgiveness from his father. When the family heard about Shavod's fatal accident, Conor asked his schoolteacher, 'Can we pray for the boy who shot my Dad?'

In the New Testament, the apostle Peter asks Jesus how many times he must forgive those who offend him, 'as many as seven times?' Jesus responds, 'I tell you, not seven times, but seventy times seven'. Steven McDonald didn't just forgive that teenager once. He forgave him over and over again, and that's because every day he woke up, he felt nothing below his neck. Each day he could only breathe thanks to a ventilator. It took him hours to have a bowel movement. Anywhere he went was by wheelchair with a nurse at his side.

In other words, Steven McDonald's wounds and his pain did not go away. He was always in pain and his physical condition always reminded him of what had happened. He was never again able to have an intimate physical relationship with his wife. He could never embrace his own son. He could never distinguish between heat and cold. He couldn't even scratch his own head.

The words of Cardinal O'Connor became true. Steven McDonald forgave and he became for that reason 'the most powerful man in the world'. He also met many other powerful men – the Pope, Nelson Mandela, and the President of the USA. Steven was so powerful because forgiveness demanded so much from him. It was not a once-off act; instead, he had to renew it each day of his life, and this was what made his spirit so powerful and strong. As he himself said, 'No human being can come to forgiveness without God. I can accept or reject that grace any day. Pray that I will accept it every day.'

One day Steven received a letter from a young woman. Her home had been burned down and everyone else in her family killed, but she had heard about how Steven McDonald forgave and she decided to do the same.

At the end of a talk Steven gave in a high school in New York, a boy asked, 'How could you forgive someone who's done this to you? I couldn't.'

Steven replied, 'When I was shot, I was dying, and my family and I said all sorts of prayers. I wanted to be forgiven then for my sins, and if I was to be forgiven by God, I had to forgive Shavod Jones. It hasn't always been easy to do that, but if I'm going to live my faith, and if I want to get to heaven, this is what I must do.'

In the summer of 2004, I spent a few weeks in the Jesuit community at Boston College. Steven's son Conor was applying to Boston College. Fr Peter Le Jacq, chaplain to the NYPD, asked me to give him and his father a tour of the campus. I was only too happy to do so. It was a privilege to encounter these two men: the father who knew in his heart that the highest form of love is forgiveness, and the son who was learning so much from his example.

Steven once said in an interview, 'The only thing worse than receiving a bullet in my spine would have been to nurture revenge in my heart. Such an attitude would have extended my injury to my soul, hurting my wife, son and others even more. It's bad enough that the physical effects are permanent, but at least I can choose to prevent spiritual injury.'

Conor went on to study at Boston College. After graduation, he entered the NYPD, just like his father. As for Steven, although the doctors had initially given him only two years to live, he survived for more than thirty years, eventually dying in January 2017. His wife Patti Ann said afterwards, 'I truly believe he is in a better place. He's not suffering or in pain. He's walking and he's free.'

Father, it's not easy for me to forgive. So many questions and objections arise in my heart: why should I be the first to reach out? Am I letting people walk all over me? Shouldn't I stand my ground? Not now, maybe later.

Basically, all these misgivings show me that I don't have the strength to live as Jesus did. Since I cannot find any real love in my heart for those who have hurt me, all I have to give you is the very misery of my angers and resentments. My hope is that by offering these wounds and resentments to you, a space will be cleared for you to move and act in my heart. And even if these wounds of mine never entirely disappear, at least with your help they won't rule my actions. You are God, and because of that I trust that you will make them life-giving, like the glorious wounds of your risen Son Jesus.

An Outstanding Witness to Forgiveness

On Sunday the 6 July 1902, the eleven-year-old Maria Goretti died of the injuries she received the previous day when she was stabbed repeatedly by a nineteen-year-old youth, while rejecting his sexual advances. As his weapon, Alessandro Serenelli had used an awl, a sharp tool for punching holes in leather. Maria, or Marietta as her family and friends called her, had been stabbed fourteen times, and left lying in a pool of blood. The awl had penetrated her throat, her back, and there was damage to her diaphragm, her lungs and even to her heart.

She went through additional torture as the horse-drawn ambulance that carried her on the seven-mile journey to hospital jolted over rough and uneven roads. Her suffering didn't finish when she arrived at hospital; her mangled body was in such a terrible state that the doctors couldn't use any anaesthetic for the two-hour operation. Even after surgery, her agony wasn't over. She continued to suffer all through Saturday night, Sunday morning and into Sunday afternoon, and she eventually died shortly before four o'clock. But well before Marietta breathed her last, she said about her attacker, 'For the love of Jesus I forgive him … and I want him to be with me in paradise'.

At first Alessandro didn't show any signs of repentance, and he was sentenced to thirty years imprisonment with hard labour. He eventually repented after a dream in which Maria appeared to him with a bouquet of fourteen lilies – one for each wound he had inflicted upon her. When he was finally released from prison, Alessandro arrived one day at the door of Maria's mother Assunta, begging her forgiveness. Assunta forgave him from the depths of her heart. In 1950, Alessandro attended Maria's canonisation ceremony in Rome, sitting next to her mother Assunta. He later became the gardener and doorkeeper at a Capuchin monastery and died in 1970.

We all experience conflicts and divisions, most of them less tragic than what Maria Goretti had to undergo. Friendships break down, marriages unravel, and many are left with huge emotional wounds. To realize that an eleven-year-old girl was able to forgive her killer is a tremendous inspiration for us adults.

There is a famous prayer of St Ignatius of Loyola that can help us to forgive. It is in his *Spiritual Exercises*, and is called 'Take Lord, receive'. Many people have a problem with this prayer: they baulk at the opening line which invites God to 'receive all my liberty, my memory, my understanding, and my entire will'. As someone said,

'If God is going to take my memory, does that mean I'll be only left with Alzheimer's?'

I understand this prayer of St Ignatius in a much more positive light. When I ask God to take my memory, I'm asking God to take away my way of remembering things and to replace it with his way of remembering. I'm asking God to change the way I remember the past, so that from now on I can look back on my past as God does. When God looks at my past, God sees his love at work in my life. If I can receive the grace to see my past as God does, then a shaft of light will appear even in the darkest hours, because God has the power to kindle a fire even within my darkest night. And so, I can be graced to become a little bit more forgiving, a little bit more like the great St Maria of Goretti.

Take Lord, receive, all my liberty, my memory, my understanding, and my entire will, all that I have and possess. You have given all to me. To you, O Lord, I return it. All is yours, dispose of it wholly according to your will. Give me only your love and your grace; that's enough for me.

Priests Should Practise Forgiveness

Maria Simma was an Austrian mystic who died in 2004. She grew up in a staunch Catholic family in the small village of Sonntag in the mountainous region of Vorarlberg, the westernmost state of Austria. She prayed a lot for the souls in purgatory. At the age of twenty-five, she began to receive visitations from these souls.

The following story, which is attributed to her, may or may not be genuine. The point it makes about forgiveness and mercy is true. Maria was asked to identify the whereabouts of two recently deceased persons. After asking the holy souls, she said that the woman, after a short stay in purgatory, was now in heaven, whereas the man would be spending a long time in purgatory before he got to paradise. The person who sought this information reacted indignantly, saying, 'You must be a liar, because that woman was a prostitute, and she died immediately after throwing herself in front of a train. But the man in question was a priest whom everyone in our village respected for his holiness.'

Maria was taken aback by this, and the next time the holy souls visited her, she voiced her misgivings. 'How come this woman, despite being a known prostitute, is in heaven after only a brief stay in purgatory, whereas the priest is due to remain in purgatory for a long time?'

The holy souls explained that although this priest was devout, he was also severe and unforgiving toward anyone who came to his confessional. In the case of this particular woman, he went so far as to refuse her a Christian burial. As for the woman herself, she underwent a real conversion just before her death. As she fell down in front of the oncoming train, she said, 'My God, at least I will no longer offend you'. Although she had become entangled in a life of sin, in her heart she loved God enough not to want to offend him anymore. God took this desire of hers seriously. Her expression of loving sorrow was enough to save her and remit practically all the punishment due for her sins, which was why she was taken up to heaven so quickly.

God's mercy and justice are both at work in this story. Despite everything she had done, this woman still loved God. She expressed her deep sorrow as best she could, and God was happy with what she gave him. She didn't judge others. She resembled the tax collector in Luke's parable who simply says, 'God, have mercy on me, a sinner' (Lk 18:13).

The priest in the story, although undoubtedly a good man, was more interested in dispensing justice than in being merciful. He resembled the Pharisee in that same parable from the Gospel of Luke, who said: 'God, I thank you that I am not like other people: rogues, adulterers' (Lk 18:11).

Let us pray that we may experience the sacrament of reconciliation with renewed depth, to taste the forgiveness and infinite mercy of God. And let us pray that God may give his Church merciful priests and not torturers (Pope Francis).

Chapter Eight

Lead Us Not into Temptation

*Everyone thinks of changing the world, but no
one thinks of changing himself.*
Leo Tolstoy

God Doesn't Tempt Us
'Well, here's another nice mess you've gotten me into.' This is
the most recognisable line from the Laurel and Hardy series
of films. Every time that Stan gets Ollie into a spot of bother,
which happens more often than not, Ollie is wont to utter these
memorable words.

The problem with the petition 'lead us not into temptation' is that
it can give the mistaken impression that God is trying to get us into
a spot of bother, a 'nice mess', by tempting us. In reality, nothing
could be further from the truth. God is not out to trip us up; God is
not out to get us. The Letter of James could not be clearer, 'No one,
when tempted, should say, "I am being tempted by God," for God
cannot be tempted by evil and he himself tempts no one' (Jas 1:13).
The words 'lead us not into temptation' do *not* mean that God is
intent on tempting us, unless we plead with him to the contrary. As
a matter of fact, the true meaning is quite different. It is something
like this, 'Don't allow us to be overcome by temptation, don't allow
us to succumb'. God does not lead us into temptation; God gives us
leadership (fatherly help) when we're in temptation.

At the same time, God is not going to fix things so that we
will escape temptation. None of us is exempt from the struggles
and trials that form part of the human condition. Everyone gets
tempted; even Jesus, the Son of God, had to undergo temptation.
However, there is something we can and should ask for when
temptation comes, as it certainly will: the strength to overcome it.

116

When we're faced with challenging moments in our lives, we're asking something like this of the Father, 'Please don't let us away from your side when we're tempted. Please keep us close to your heart, because we're not strong enough to protect ourselves.'

Although we cannot escape temptation and cannot surmount it on our own, there are a couple of things we can do. We can avoid the kinds of situations that provoke us to do wrong. We can be especially vulnerable to wrongdoing in certain circumstances, either because of our particular temperament or on account of the natural weakness we have as part of our human nature. These kinds of situations are traditionally called 'occasions of sin'.

Millions of people have heard Leonard Cohen's iconic song 'Hallelujah', which describes how King David was bowled over by the beauty of a woman he saw bathing on the roof. The Second Book of Samuel gives a more detailed account, showing how David did anything but avoid the occasion of sin. It may have all begun with David shirking his duty. Although he was a formidable warrior, he stayed back in Jerusalem while his army went off to battle. He wasn't pressured by affairs of state at the time. In fact, while his men went off to fight, David spent most of the day doing effectively nothing – he stayed in bed, only getting up when evening came.

He then went onto the roof of his royal palace, from which he would have had a commanding view of the dwellings below. Standing on the roof, he spotted a woman bathing below, probably in an open courtyard. He was struck by the woman's beauty. David could have stopped things then and there by averting his eyes. He could have exercised self-control, and easily nipped this temptation in the bud. Instead, he kept staring at her, and then sent someone to find out who the woman was. The man explained that she was Bathsheba, the wife of Uriah the Hittite. Now, David knew she was a married woman, but this didn't stop him. He took another step, by sending messengers to have her brought to him. At that time, when messengers arrived to bring a woman to see the king, she didn't have much choice – the king's will had to be obeyed. After she was brought to him, David slept with her, and Bathsheba became pregnant as a result.

When it comes to avoiding occasions of sin, we need to be honest about our own limitations. Like King David, we can too easily place ourselves in a compromising situation because we convince ourselves that we're 'above' doing wrong in that particular situation.

Another help in the face of temptation is not to give in to worry or anxiety. Temptations of one kind or another are here to stay. Don't panic when you're tempted; don't tell yourself: 'This is horrendous, I can't go on anymore'. Try saying, 'This is difficult, but it's not the end of the world and I'm not going to lose my peace of mind on account of it. Getting anxious won't fix things.' Sometimes you find yourself asking, 'I'm doing my level best, how come temptations are increasing?' We hold on to the illusory hope that the more we grow as God's children, the less temptations we'll have to face. In fact, the more we advance, the more temptations there are, and the more aggressive they become.

It's not a sin to be tempted. If temptations hurt you, the wounds can never cut through to your soul. The Lord stitched you together in your mother's womb; despite the pain, these wounds cannot unstitch you. A soldier is happy for others to see his battle scars so they can honour his courage. In the spiritual struggle, your wounds honour your bravery and fortitude. They remind you of everything you have overcome to get to where you are today. They remind you that without them, you would never have become the person you are now. They show how you stood firm through the difficult hours. They encourage you to remain as strong and courageous as you have always been. Your wounds are your badge of honour.

Lord Jesus, as the end of your life on earth approached, you wanted to reassure your disciples. You told them they would face challenging times ahead. Yet you also comforted them with these words: 'I have said this to you so that in me you may have peace. In the world you face persecution, but take courage: I have conquered the world!' (Jn 16:33).

My heart is easily troubled by the storms of life, and too often I give in to fear. You don't want me to live with an anxious heart. Please give me your peace.

Watch and Pray

Jesus had a clear sense of purpose in everything he did. It's not as though he needed to listen to the scribes or Pharisees to know what his goal was. He already had the clarity he needed, the clarity of love. In everything he did there was always a lesson for us. When he was tempted in the desert, the evil one was only able to approach him at the end of an extended period of prayer and fasting. Through this timing, the Lord was telling us that prayer and fasting ward off temptation.

The importance of fasting from food should not be exaggerated. In fact, refraining from bad-mouthing people is a much more important kind of fasting. But for all that, abstaining from food still has its place, as long as we do it in the right spirit and with the right motivation. If we use fasting to receive the adulation of others or to show how proud we are of our own humility, we're wasting our time. There is a place, however, for the kind of fasting that draws us closer to God. True fasting is not so much about saying no to food as it is about saying yes to our longing for God: it is about getting in touch with our deep, inner hunger for the Lord. Fasting is not a means to earn God's grace, something that is in any case impossible. God's grace is always gratuitous and unearned. True fasting opens us up to God's loving voice, so that God's power can work in our lives. God is constantly speaking to us, but there are so many other voices around that we often don't hear him. Through fasting we can become more attuned to his voice, because our spiritual antennae become sharpened.

On the last evening of his life, Jesus warned his disciples to be vigilant in the face of temptation. On this occasion, in the Garden of Gethsemane, he didn't mention fasting. He underlined the importance of watching and praying, advising Peter, James, and John to: 'watch and pray so that you will not fall into temptation' (Mt 26:41). But the disciples did not take in the significance of these words: 'watch and pray', and so they succumbed to drowsiness and dozed off. They did not realise that without prayer it was impossible to stay spiritually awake, and so when the guards arrived to arrest Jesus, they scattered like cowards.

119

We can fall spiritually asleep as well. Our prayer, which is intended to bring us closer to God, can unravel into an empty babbling or a mechanical drill. The ardour and passion of our initial love for God can degenerate into a mindless mediocrity. Instead of making the effort to swim against the tide, we can resign ourselves to drifting with the current. We can end up following the crowd, allowing our lives be dragged down to the level of the lowest common denominator.

If we don't make the effort to renew our love for God daily, we will become more and more lukewarm. And the more we sink into the slumber of mediocrity, the more fearful we will be of meeting Jesus on the way of the Cross. We need the vigilance of prayer to regain our spiritual consciousness. Prayer rouses us from the triviality of an existence that is centred upon ourselves. Prayer reminds us that we cannot dream our way to the truth, and in the process, prayer gives us the courage to fight the good fight and finish the race.

Father, I'd love for you to find me fully awake. But so often I'm drowsy and discouraged, a mixture of good intentions and constant distractions. Take me as I am Lord, but don't let me stay as I am. Raise me above my mediocrity and make of me everything that you want me to be.

Vigilance in Sight and Speech

We can practise vigilance especially in terms of sight and speech. Vigilance of the eyes is not just about avoiding lustful glances; it's about averting our gaze from anything that harms the soul. A tiny speck of dirt can lead to huge irritation in the bodily eye; the eye of the soul is even more sensitive to anything unclean. Our eyes belong to us, they are in our custody; they are not run by TikTok, YouTube or any other entity or group. We effectively surrender that custody to whatever we allow ourselves to see, whether it's a trashy TV programme or a shady website.

Vigilance of the tongue reminds us not to talk too much and not to use harmful or unhelpful words. Words can be destructive. We all know that technology has given bullies a much wider platform through online name-calling, and we know this can emotionally destroy children and teenagers. As a child, I repeated the nursery rhyme, 'Sticks and stones may break my bones, but words will never hurt me'. Back then, I unthinkingly accepted the truth of this phrase. Now that I'm an adult, I see how intimidating the world of childhood has become, because of things like cyber-bullying. Words can be used as weapons. They can be as sharp as knives, or even sharper: the pen is mightier than the sword.

Words can cause irreparable damage. Now I have rewritten the second half of this nursery rhyme, 'Sticks and stones may break my bones, but words will *really* hurt me'. The reason words can unleash such havoc is because words are extraordinarily powerful, 'How great a forest is set ablaze by a such a small fire! And the tongue is a fire' (Jas 3:5–6).

Words are not only destructive, they are also creative.

The unique overflowing, sparkling, self-giving, life-giving Divine Word is mirrored in myriad ways in our life-giving human words. When we speak creative words, it is as though Christ were really speaking in us.

The gift of speech is the most useful gift that God has given us. With this gift, we can turn to God in praise and thanksgiving, we can make God known and loved to those around us; we can reassure them, raise their spirits, and express our affection for them. How can we use this amazing gift for the good? The answer isn't self-evident. Our parents and our teachers taught us how to speak and how to recite the alphabet. They explained the rules of grammar and showed us how to put sentences together, but they did not say much about the power of words.

The Book of Proverbs tells us, 'Death and life are in the power of the tongue' (Prov 18:21). In case this sentence from Scripture sounds far-fetched, here are two concrete examples. In countries where the death penalty still exists, the words of a judge can result in the execution of an accused person. Later the convicted person may be shown clemency through the words of a president or head of state. On the other hand, a doctor can speak life-giving words, by suggesting surgery that might cure someone with a terminal illness.

Words do not just bring physical death or life. They can also kill the soul or make it blossom like a flower. Someone can speak words that have the power to kill your dream, words such as, 'You'll never amount to anything!' Yet words can also transform your life, such as these three words, 'I love you'.

We need to surprise ourselves and others with creative words that connect us to our greatest hopes and desires. We need words that open us up to the unvisited layers of our own humanity. We need to learn to talk as though it were for the first time – all over again.

Ultimately all the best sounds emerge from a deep well of silence, a well that has been washed clean of internal chatter as well as external words. It's only from the stillness of this deep well that we begin to notice how much of what we had planned to say doesn't really need to be said at all. As a counterbalance to the noisiness of our world, it may just be worth refraining from speech unless we can improve upon silence.

Father, I'm full of buzzing thoughts and noisy words. Please, create within me a zone of stillness. Help me find the silence that helps me find myself. I'm fed up of achieving; give me the openness to receive. I've grasped too much at things; may I be grasped instead by the wonder of your creation. I'm tense from holding on; teach me how to let go. I want to celebrate you, your goodness and your gifts; not in order to get a reward, but simply for the joy it brings you.

Humbly Asking for Help

I remember the day I entered the Church of the Nativity in Bethlehem. It was a 'belittling' experience, in the best sense of the word. The entrance couldn't have been more than five feet high. In order to fit through its small frame, I had to lower not just my eyes, but my whole body; a profound bow was literally unavoidable. The Door of Humility is the name given to this tiny entrance to the church where Jesus was born. Perhaps there is a valuable lesson in this experience of being cut down to size: only the truly humble can draw close to God.

The petition 'lead us not into temptation' is the request of a humble person. Humility doesn't mean pretending you're stupid if in fact you're intelligent, or convincing yourself that you're ugly when in reality you're good looking. What it does mean is recognising that your intelligence and good looks are not things to boast about, since they are *gifts*. Humility is truth, and the truth is that as well as being blessed in so many ways, each of us is only a tiny speck in a gigantic universe, even if we like to picture ourselves at its centre. We are infinitesimally small in relation to the infinite. We are so limited in so many ways that it doesn't make sense to exalt ourselves above others, simply because we have received certain blessings that they don't have.

As Michel de Montaigne once pointed out, even if we find ourselves on the highest throne in the world, we're still only sitting on our own bottoms! Humble people know themselves for what they are. Some of us may strut about and blow our own trumpets, but the humbling truth is that all of us emerged out of nothingness. The humble cast aside the illusion that they can do it all by themselves. Even if we become big shots, the sobering truth is that we can be killed by a virus so tiny that it is invisible to the naked eye. Humble people admit that their take on things is pretty limited. Socrates, the ancient Greek philosopher, was declared the wisest man in Athens, precisely because he knew how ignorant he was. The humble realise that they don't know everything, and so they're open to asking new questions, to growing and developing and to expanding their horizons. Humble people acknowledge that they are far from being as good as they would like to be. They realise that despite their desire to act well, they don't always succeed. As St Paul once said, 'For I do not do the good I want, but the evil I do not want is what I do' (Rom 7:19).

Fundamentally, if you are humble, you own up to the truth that you are not God. As a spiritual guru once said, 'There is good news and there is better news. The good news is that there is a Messiah; the better news is that it's not you!' To admit that you are not God is to confess the truth. Because it is the truth, it should not lead to a loss of trust or to a sense of despair. The good thief did not despair. Instead of focusing on himself, he turned his eyes to the Lord and said, 'Jesus, remember me when you come into your kingdom' (Lk 23:42). Although his hands and feet were tied to a cross, his heart was free, because it moved him to abandon himself to the goodness and mercy of Jesus.

People who admit the truth about themselves – about their strengths and weaknesses, their successes and failures – are humble enough to reach out in trust to others. When it comes to God, there are even greater reasons for trust, because God is as solid as a rock, as reliable as you can get.

Father, when I'm tempted, draw me close to you so that in my moments of weakness I may find your strength, and when I risk becoming enslaved, you will guide me in the opposite direction, the best road of all, the one that leads to freedom.

The Lure of Temptation

Homer's epic Greek poem *The Odyssey* was a popular tale in the ancient Mediterranean world. It is the story of the warrior Odysseus's journey back home to the island of Ithaca after the Trojan War. In Book 12 of the *Odyssey*, Odysseus and his crew of sailors encounter the Sirens, mythical creatures whose irresistible singing voices entice sailors to their death. The enchanting song of the Sirens shows why temptation is so difficult to resist. We're not drawn by repulsive and repellent things, but by the allure of attractive and appealing things. The beguiling singing of the Sirens promises something without any foundation, and if Odysseus and his men give in, their ship will shatter on the rocks. In a similar way, if we succumb to the empty promise of temptation, it will lead to moral shipwreck.

Odysseus is humble enough to realise that he and his men will be unable to resist the seductive songs of the Sirens. He has them fill their ears with beeswax so that they won't hear the music. He has them tie him so securely to the mast of the boat that he won't be able to break free. Thanks to these measures, they manage to resist temptation. The oarsmen cannot hear the Sirens, while Odysseus is unable to respond to their bewitching singing because he cannot release himself from the ropes that bind him and his men are deaf to his pleas. In this episode, Odysseus recognises that he needs help; in the Lord's Prayer we also ask for help not to succumb.

Jesus calls the devil the 'father of lies' (Jn 8:44) and St Paul warns that the evil one 'disguises himself as an angel of light' (2 Cor 11:14), so it's not surprising that temptation, deceptive as it is, holds a huge allure. The story of Adam and Eve's fall from grace illustrates this particularly well.

At the start of this fateful story, Eve is already near the tree of the knowledge of good and evil, a tree about which God has warned Adam and herself. In a similar way, we often place ourselves unnecessarily close to situations of temptation. While she is there, a snake starts speaking to her. This bizarre event should already raise the alarm in her mind. Animals certainly emits cries and sounds, but they don't speak words that we can understand. God has told them to beware of the tree of the knowledge of good and evil, so Eve should be especially wary when she comes across a speaking snake near this suspicious tree. But it seems as though this odd creature simply piques her curiosity. Perhaps she's thinking: 'Awesome! Wait until I tell Adam about this talkative snake!'

God is not far away; in fact, he walks in the garden in the cool of the evening. Eve could easily call out to him, and ask him to tell her more about this puzzling snake. Instead of turning with confidence to God, she puts her faith in the words of this weird snake.

The snake's opening question contains a huge lie. He asks, 'Did God say, "You shall not eat from any tree in the garden"?' (Gen 3:1). God did *not* say anything of the sort. God did not stop Adam and Eve from eating the fruit of any tree in the garden. God did the opposite: he encouraged them to eat from every tree in the garden, save one. Apart from one specific tree, every other tree was theirs. The snake's question gives the impression that God has created this lush garden filled with beautiful trees, only to forbid Adam and Eve from tasting the fruit of any of its trees. He implies that God is stern, severe and even sadistic.

Eve defends God, explaining that they are allowed eat of the fruit of any tree in the garden, apart from the fruit of the tree in the middle of the garden. By means of his question, the snake has focused her attention on the one thing forbidden to her, the fruit of the tree of the knowledge of good and evil. She forgets the enormous blessings – the fact that she may eat the fruit of every other tree in the garden. In a similar way, we can find ourselves annoyed at some little thing we lack instead of being grateful for the enormous gifts with which we have been blessed.

God warned Adam and Eve that eating the forbidden fruit would lead to their death. The snake alleges the exact opposite: if they eat this fruit, they will become more alive than they could ever imagine. In fact, he suggests that God himself is afraid of them, because he realizes that by eating this fruit, Adam and Eve will become like him, knowing good and evil. The snake wants her to grab whatever she can in a proud way, instead of accepting everything she already has in a humble manner.

He urges Eve not to accept that this particular tree is off limits. Yet this limitation is for the benefit of Adam and Eve; it's a gift, not an imposition. A sign near a steep cliff saying, 'keep away' is to our advantage, not to our detriment. Human beings cannot fly: this is part of our limitation. If we fall off a steep cliff, we will be injured or die. God's command is not a restriction on Eve's freedom but a gift that enhances it.

God isn't refusing knowledge of good and evil to Adam and Eve, but he wants them to arrive at this knowledge without eating the forbidden fruit. By giving in to temptation, they will come to know good and evil as the slaves of evil. By not eating the forbidden fruit, they would come to know good and evil as victors over temptation.

The fruit appears to be good food, a delight for the eyes and a stepping stone to wisdom. Eve forgets that she already enjoys good food that is a delight for the eyes – the fruit of every other tree in the garden. Moreover, she already possesses wisdom. The snake fools her into thinking that she will magically arrive at a godlike knowledge if she partakes of this fruit.

Once she eats of the fruit and persuades Adam to do the same, everything changes, but not in the way the snake promised. Although they were already naked, now this reality makes them ashamed. As long as their relationship with God was transparent, their nakedness and vulnerability were not threatening. Now they cannot even be open with one another, and try to conceal their rising shame under the cover of fig leaves. The snake promised they would know good and evil; that much is true. But this new knowledge does not make them like God, despite the assurances of the snake. In fact, it has the opposite effect, making them more unlike God than ever before.

Father, Adam and Eve succumbed to temptation, yet you brought good out of that sad situation, by sending your Son among us to bring us back to you. In my own life, I often lose hope when I make yet another mistake. Grant that I may rise above discouragement at those difficult moments. If you could transform the fall of Adam and Eve into something glorious, I dare to believe that you can make good the mishaps and misadventures in my little life.

The Temptation not to Become a Full Christian

Teenagers often experience life as something that simply happens. Parents tell them to settle down and do something with their lives. This pressure to make definitive choices doesn't appeal to them. They prefer to wait and see what happens. They become excited about a person or a cause for a while, and then move on to something else. In young adulthood, there usually comes a point where they no longer sit back and let life flow by; now they decide to set about making something of their lives, in a conscious and intentional way. It's like the difference between falling in love, which happens, and staying in love, which demands a real choice.

Something similar happens in the world of faith. We imagine that we're Christians because we go to church, know the rituals and are in tune with religious language. But clinging to inherited practices is not enough to fill the empty space inside: sooner or later the light will grow dimmer until it final goes out. We need to cultivate a relationship with Jesus Christ that lives up to our adult experience. And this kind of relationship won't happen unless we make it happen.

Sometimes even years of regular prayer and dedicated service aren't enough. After all this giving, we can still find ourselves assailed by doubts and questions. As the years go by, core principles in our faith can threaten to totter and fall. Meanwhile, old passions come back to haunt us, passions we thought were long ago resolved. This onset of confusion and darkness can be especially worrying for those who have always regarded themselves as committed Christians. They plunged into the Christian experience from the start, and imagined that all they needed to do over time was to strengthen and deepen their initial commitment. They didn't bargain with a complete transformation: 'unless a grain of wheat falls into the ground and dies, it remains a single grain' (Jn 12:24). In this verse from John's Gospel, Jesus says that a new kind of life only comes about if we first die. It's not about becoming bigger and better versions of ourselves; it's about dying to ourselves in order to be born anew.

This transformation must be more than skin deep; it needs to touch the heart. The inner world with its contrasting movements of warm love and icy indifference can be hugely intimidating. We often prefer to ignore the deep feelings that surge inside of us. It is only through paying attention to our feelings, memories and dreams that we can become aware of how light and darkness are at work in our lives.

The kinds of experiences that unlock the door to our affective life are often crisis moments such as sickness, unemployment, or the breakup of a relationship. We can run away from these trials or we can use them as springboards to plunge more deeply into who we are with all our ambiguities. We are only brave when we have learned to face our fears. We are only loving when we have withstood the temptation to hate. We are only strong when we have acknowledged our weakness.

Father, help me learn to live compassionately with my fragility by looking at how Jesus did it. Give me fresh eyes to gaze at Jesus as he weeps at the grave of his good friend Lazarus. Grant that I may look kindly at him in the Garden of Gethsemane as he pleads with Peter, James, and John to 'stay here and keep watch with me'. Let his words – 'I thirst' – spoken on the Cross, resonate in my heart.

Chapter Nine

Deliver Us from Evil

If only it were all so simple! If only there were evil people somewhere insidiously committing evil deeds, and it were necessary only to separate them from the rest of us and destroy them. But the line dividing good and evil cuts through the heart of every human being. And who is willing to destroy a piece of his own heart?
Alexander Solzhenitsyn

Do You Want to Be Delivered from Evil?

Weddings are enjoyable for many reasons. It's not just because of the chance to dress up and enjoy a lot of free food – and drink! There are deeper reasons: the wonder of witnessing two people who freely choose to spend their lives together. Their commitment gets us thinking about what we're doing with our own lives. We even find ourselves believing in love once again, at least for a day!

I'm always gobsmacked by the words said by the bride and groom as they exchange vows. They promise to stay together as husband and wife, 'for better, for worse, for richer, for poorer, in sickness and in health' all the days of their lives. These words display an extraordinary level of commitment to each other.

A bride and groom are basically saying that in order to stay together, they are ready to put up with poverty, ill-health and all sorts of adverse circumstances. The worst evil would be separation from one another.

In practice we often see the shortage of money or the lack of health as the real evils. These are certainly challenging realities, but are they as bad as they appear? A couple getting married proclaim before witnesses that the real evil is to lose their love and drift away from each other. In the life of a Christian, evil is whatever separates us from God and makes us less generous in his service.

Jesus said, 'Blessed are the poor in spirit'. To be poor in spirit is to be free of fixation on money and possessions. This obsession with wealth can afflict the poor as well as the rich. The rich can become attached to money; the poor can curse and hate those who have more than they do. By failing to be poor in spirit, we fail to remember the profound truth of which the Episcopalian priest, John Heuss, has reminded us, 'People were created to be loved. Things were created to be used. Most of our troubles come from the fact that we love things and use people.'

The following story brings this truth home. It's a story that has become widely diffused in different versions on the internet. It was originally composed by a famous writer who bought a house on Achill Island in 1958 and lived there on and off until he died in 1985. He won the Nobel Prize for Literature in 1972. His name was Heinrich Böll. A year before Böll bought his house on Achill Island, he published a book about Ireland – *Irisches Tagebuch* (Irish Diary) – that sold over two million copies in Germany alone. It has shaped the German perception of Ireland ever since.

The particular story I want to re-tell was written by Böll for a German radio programme in 1973, the year after he had been awarded the Nobel Prize. The story recounts an intriguing encounter between a businessman on holidays and a small fisherman in an out-of-the-way harbour on the west coast of Europe. Böll does not name the exact location, but given his love for the west of Ireland, I think we can make an educated guess that the story may in fact be set there.

So, let's say a tourist is walking through the village of Roundstone in Connemara when he notices a fisherman reclining in his boat, taking in the warm afternoon sun. The tourist is taken aback to see the man isn't working.

The tourist stops and says, 'You won't catch any fish if you stay like that'. The fisherman gives him a quizzical look. The tourist continues, 'Don't just sit there, do something!'

The fisherman replies, 'And what would I get if I did something?'

'You'd get more money, and you could then buy bigger nets and catch plenty of fish!' says the tourist enthusiastically.

'And what would I get if I did that?' the fisherman asks.

The tourist replies, 'You'd get enough money to buy a proper motor for your boat'.

'And what would I get if I did that?' asks the fisherman, smiling gently.

'Well, you'd soon have enough money to buy a whole fleet of boats', says the tourist.

'And what would I get if I did that?' the fisherman wonders out loud, smiling.

By this stage the tourist is becoming irritated by the fisherman's laid-back attitude. He feels the fisherman isn't taking his advice seriously.

'Don't you get it?' he shouts. 'Within a couple of years, you'd have a whole fleet of boats, then you could open a fish restaurant, and before you know it, you'd be overseeing a huge company, whizzing around from one place to another in your private helicopter.'

Once again, the fisherman asks, 'And what would I get if I did that?'

By this time the tourist has become livid with rage. 'You really don't get it, do you? This is what you would get – you would get so much money that you'd never have to work again. You could simply take it easy, sit by the harbour and gaze at the setting sun. You wouldn't have a worry in the world!'

A big smile lit up the fisherman's face as he said, 'And what do you think I'm doing right now?'

What a story! As Jesus might have said, 'Blessed is that fisherman'. The tourist felt the fisherman was losing out, yet the fisherman himself saw his life in a much more positive light. It would have taken a huge amount of work – and stress – to arrive at a state that the fisherman was already enjoying without any stress at all. The tourist was pushing the fisherman to make as much money as possible so that he could finally retire and enjoy life – but by that stage he would have probably been too stressed and frustrated to enjoy retirement. The frenetic search for what we don't have can divert us from being thankful for what is already ours.

*Father, I often ask to be delivered from things that are not in fact evil.
Help me to see that the real evil is any thought, word or action that
breaks the bond of love that binds me to you.*

Deliver Us from Evil Thoughts

In the early centuries of Christianity, believers suffered sporadic but
intense bouts of persecution throughout the Roman Empire. Things
changed for the better with the proclamation of the Edict of Milan
in AD 313. Christians were now free to worship and practise their
faith without fear of persecution. After being outsiders for so long,
Christians now found themselves unexpectedly feeling at home
in the world. For many of them, this newfound security did not
feel quite right. As a result, around the same time that the Roman
Empire officially became Christian, more and more Christians felt
drawn to move away from cities and seek God in the solitude of
the desert. They withdrew from the world, embraced the monastic
life, and sought God in lives of silence and prayer. The desert didn't
turn out to be a peaceful haven: it was the theatre of a new kind of
persecution, bloodless yet intense. Now that the wholesale attacks
on Christians had abated, something new gathered force: persecution by thoughts.

This kind of persecution is still ours today. A constant flow of
random thoughts pours through our minds. These are thoughts we
never wanted to entertain; they arrive unannounced and unbidden.
They focus on everything from positive memories to despairing
prospects: 'That was a great night out last week', 'I need to lose
weight', 'Will I ever amount to anything?' These thoughts can zoom
around like cars driving at breakneck speed.

Becoming aware of this stream of thoughts might not appear to
be especially helpful. After all, won't this awareness make us even
more desperate? We're afraid that becoming conscious of this endless din inside will only drive us to greater distraction. Most of us
want control more than we want awareness. We would like to stop
certain thoughts and feelings from popping up all the time. We'd
like to be able to make sure we never have such thoughts in the first

place. The truth is that this kind of thought control is out of our hands – we can't decide what thoughts are going to arise.

To become aware of these thoughts running through our heads helps us to see that many of them are not really *our* thoughts. We may never even have wanted to have such thoughts. We need to take these thoughts with a grain of salt. We burden ourselves with huge anxiety when we take our thoughts too seriously, wrongly imagining that we are our thoughts. Of themselves, these haphazard thoughts only buzz around at a superficial level. They do not reflect the deepest layer of who we are.

Father, my thoughts keep racing at breakneck speed in all directions. Suddenly I'm fixated on a problem, and before I know it, I'm drowning in negativity. Lord, help me to see that you are more lasting than my feelings and mightier than my thoughts. Unchain me from this sad merry-go-round, release me from this vicious circle. Help me to stand back from these unwelcome thoughts that hurtle along the inner race-track of my mind. Breathe peace upon my stormy interior.

Coping With Commotion

What is the nature of this inner commotion that brings such anxiety in its wake? There's a clue at the start of the Book of Genesis. It's the phrase '*tohu wa-bohu*', and it appears in the first chapter of this first book of the Bible. This Hebrew phrase has a rhyming quality and deep-sounding vowels. There is something elemental and primeval about it. 'The earth was a formless void [*tohu wa-bohu*] and darkness covered the face of the deep, and the Spirit of God moved over the face of the waters' (Gen 1:2).

At the beginning, the world was formless and void – *tohu wa-bohu*. '*Tohu*' means formless, worthless, chaos, waste, desolateness. '*Bohu*' has an essentially similar meaning; it means void, emptiness, waste. At the dawn of time there was *tohu wa-bohu*, and additionally there was darkness. The picture that is painted is bleak – formlessness, desolateness, chaos, void, and utter darkness. It has all the ingredients of a forlorn situation that is bereft of hope.

Thankfully things didn't remain stuck in the shapeless void of *tohu wa-bohu*. There was a supremely creative response to it: the Spirit *of God*, no less, moved over the face of the waters. This desolate waste didn't discourage God and this despairing scenario didn't throw him off balance. As a matter of fact, it didn't faze him in the least. On the contrary: in the face of this darkness and chaos, God acted, God did something. God moved over the face of the waters.

This is hugely encouraging. Just when the void of the *bohu* reinforces even more the emptiness of the *tohu*, just at this nadir of total hopelessness, the Spirit sets to work. This is not only good news but great news. The message is clear: whenever there is chaos, God is ready to come to the rescue. If I call out to God, he won't leave me in forlornness; he won't forget me when my life is in a mess.

When I feel desolate and empty, when I find myself in darkness and in despair, in other words, whenever I am undergoing an onslaught of *tohu wa-bohu*, I can confidently call upon the Holy Spirit. The Holy Spirit is more than ready to move over my emptiness, to sweep over my formlessness, and to draw me out of chaos into the light of meaning and hope.

Left to my own devices, a *tohu wa-bohu* experience can spell disaster. But if I ask the Holy Spirit to sweep over me, I will be ushered into the light. As the third verse of the opening chapter of Genesis says, 'Then God said, "Let there be light", and there was light' (Gen 1:3).

Father, please remind me that your Spirit can create something good out of my tohu wa-bohu, *out of the painful wounds I carry from childhood, out of the self-destructive habits I've formed, and out of the darkness I've absorbed from my culture. Holy Spirit, rescue me, create something good out of the tangled threads of my existence, rejuvenate my life so that I do not simply grow old but also become new.*

The Inner Battle between Good and Evil

There is a battle going on inside. If we stay alert and decisive, we'll arrive at the freedom of the true self. A striking example of this inner struggle is found in the story of St Ignatius of Loyola. Defeat in a physical battle led him to wake up to an even more important battle going on inside. As a result, he learned a momentous lesson that transformed his life and has inspired countless people ever since. Over five hundred years ago, in 1521, this gallant knight in armour was hit by a cannonball that shattered his leg and his dreams. Despite one agonizing operation after another, Ignatius had to spend months in bed to regain movement and flexibility in his wounded leg. During these long months, he asked for books on chivalry to pass the time. His sister-in-law had other ideas: she gave him books on the lives of the saints and the life of Jesus.

Although he was no longer a functioning soldier, a real battle developed inside Ignatius. It was a battle between two different selves, two different 'Ignatiuses', and they were truly at loggerheads. One Ignatius was mesmerised by Jesus and the saints, by their amazing freedom from power and prestige, from public opinion and possessions. The other Ignatius stubbornly refused to give up the dream of becoming a valiant knight. Again and again, Ignatius saw himself as a strong and virile hero, the knight in shining armour who would win the lady of his hopes come what may.

It was only after a period of time that Ignatius began to realise that these two conflicting dreams left him in two distinct frames of mind. The prospect of being the tough man with a magnanimous soul sent a rush of adrenaline through his veins. Crucially, the thrill did not last. It wore off more quickly than he cared to believe. And all that remained was a disheartening emptiness. However, things were different when his inner gaze turned to Jesus and the saints. The joy and attraction he felt inside did not vanish into thin air; the sense of peace remained. Slowly it dawned upon him that the abiding sense of peace was drawing him toward God, while the desires that left him dissatisfied were pulling him in the opposite direction.

In our own ways, we all experience two selves inside. There is the surface self that is focused on having things (for Ignatius it was all about having power, wealth, and a noble wife), accomplishing things (becoming the most valiant and successful knight ever), and getting approval from outside (being respected and even venerated by his peers). This false self is never secure: at any moment fame, fortune and the accolade of devotees can fade away.

Many of us experience a constant pendulum swing from one self to another. In the course of a single day, we can move from generosity (stopping to talk with a homeless man on the street and giving him spare change) to complete self-absorption (I'm text messaging and don't disturb me!) The false self promises much and delivers next to nothing: after the inevitable thrill, we're left dissatisfied. The true self imparts a joy that lasts, a sense of being at home with ourselves and the world. The false self drags us back into the past of unhealthy habits; the true self draws us forward toward a fuller life.

If you want to live in tune with who you really are, here's a vital rule to live by: resist the temptation to make big decisions when you're in a bad space. When you're in a bad space, the world looks worse than it is, just like when you're wearing sunglasses everything appears darker than it truly is.

Here's a story to make this vital point as clear as possible (names, places and certain details have been changed, but the gist of the story is true).

One morning a Jesuit priest gave a talk to some college students about how to make decisions. He kept returning to the point I just mentioned: don't make big decisions when you're in a bad zone. He added that it's precisely at such moments that we're tempted to make major decisions, because we think they are the very things that will get us out of this bad space. Often these decisions boomerang on us and make things even worse.

Several days later, one of the students came back to see him. Her name was Sarah. She said, 'Father, what you said is so true, it really works'. He said, 'What works?' 'That rule you gave us about making big decisions', Sarah replied. The priest was intrigued, 'Tell me more'. Sarah told him about her friend Aoife who had been on the point of dropping out of university.

'It was last Friday. I arrived at our flat and Aoife was packing her things. Not just a few clothes as she usually did when she was going home for the weekend. No, this time it was a real clear-out: everything was going into suitcases and travel bags. "What's the matter?" I asked her. She said, "I've had enough. I'm getting out of college". That wasn't like Aoife. I couldn't believe it. I mean, she's a star student, she's a great athlete, and she has a ton of friends. Why was she suddenly packing it all in? It just didn't make any sense. I said, "Aoife, you can't just walk out like this; you owe me an explanation". She had this really sad expression in her face. She said, "I wanted to be a doctor, but this year of pre-med is crazy: I'm two months into it, and I've just failed my first set of exams. This is new territory for me: I've never even got a B in an exam before, never mind failing. And then I texted my boyfriend to meet him for coffee, I figured he might give me some support, and two minutes later he texts me back telling me he's just met someone new. Can you believe it? He hasn't even got the guts and the decency to tell me face to face. He calls it all off with a line of stupid text. So, there you have it. In the space of an hour, I failed my exams and my boyfriend failed me. That's why I'm going."'

Sarah immediately thought of the rule about big decisions. She pleaded with Aoife, 'Please don't do this now, not when you're so upset'. Aoife replied, 'Well, what do you want me to do, wait around until I'm even more upset?' Sarah replied, 'Listen, come down with me to Wexford for the weekend. We'll book into a B & B. I'll just meet you for breakfast and in the evenings. Otherwise, take time out, walk along the beach, look at the waves and relax. We'll drive back up to Dublin on Sunday evening. And then if you still feel the same way you do now, I'll help you carry all those bags out the door on Monday morning.'

Aoife agreed. On Sunday evening as they drove back to Dublin, Aoife said, 'Thanks so much for the weekend. You know, it was while I was looking out to sea this afternoon that it suddenly hit me: I don't want to be a doctor at all. It was my mother who was pushing me to do it. She has been pushing me so much and for so long that I began to believe that I wanted it too. But you know, I don't want it at all. It's stories and novels that have always fascinated me. I'm going to give up medicine. I'm going to switch to English literature.' She stopped for a moment to clear her throat. 'And as for that boyfriend, although my head told me that he ticked all the right boxes, my heart has been telling me for the last two months to run away from him, but I never stopped long enough to listen to it. I'm better off without him.' As Sarah parked the car, Aoife gave her a big smile and said, 'I'm staying at UCD'.

Sarah took the key from the ignition and put on the handbrake. Although a few drops of rain were tapping on the windscreen outside, inside the car a sense of peace and stillness reigned. Sarah felt so happy that she held Aoife in a long embrace. The tears rolled down their faces. As Sarah finished telling this story to the Jesuit priest, she said, 'That rule about not making a big decision from a bad space is so important. If Aoife had left college last Friday, her whole life would have collapsed around her.'

Sarah saved Aoife from a lot of unnecessary unhappiness. Unfortunately, too many people make too many decisions from an unhelpful space inside themselves. They walk out of marriages because they're feeling down. They turn to someone new just to fill the gnawing dissatisfaction they feel inside. They make major life changes when they are full of anxiety and in no proper state of mind to do so.

So, please follow this basic wisdom in your life too. When you feel out of tune with yourself and others and God, you'll also find that you're blown this way and that by moods and feelings, and they'll often urge you to make a big decision. But if you're feeling that uneasy with life and with yourself, it's the worst time to make a major move. Don't get hijacked by your surface self! Wait! Be patient! In the meantime, while you're waiting and exercising your patience, share your pain with someone you trust, turn to friends for support and ask God to help and heal you – you'll be glad you did.

Father, in the course of a single day, I find myself moving between two quite different selves. The self I'm not particularly fond of is the 'look-at-me-self'. It's a self that always tries to impress others and please them. But there's also a deeper self, the 'wondrous child', full of a sense of awe before you and others. It's a child that trusts its own feelings and doesn't need to win the love of others through performing. The only thing is – I can't hold onto this good self for long. Sooner or later, the wondrous child

139

sinks under the weight of everyday hassles. But at least, thanks to your light, I've begun to realise that I can live more and more from this deeper source within me.

Opposing Evil in a Peaceful Way

From the beginning, spiritual masters have realised that the real battle is an inside battle, going on within each human heart. The first important figure to write about this inner battle was Evagrius of Pontus. Born in the middle of the fourth century, Evagrius withdrew to the Egyptian desert and became an outstanding spiritual guide. He wrote a manual called *Talking Back* (*Antirrhetikos*), in which he explained how to fight successfully against unhelpful thoughts. Taking his cue from Jesus, who used the words of Scripture to withstand the temptations of the devil in the desert, Evagrius listed almost 500 passages from the Bible. He arranged these passages topically, according to whether the particular temptation was gluttony, the love of money, anger, pride, or something else. These biblical passages were to be learned by heart, and used as spiritual armour against the enemy of our human nature.

What can we learn from spiritual guides such as Evagrius of Pontus? That if we're trying to lead a spiritual life, we'll be drawn into spiritual warfare. This warfare takes the form of a battle against evil thoughts. What takes getting used to is the fact that this battle is invisible: we cannot see our thoughts. Many of us have watched so many action movies that we think of battles as visible and even spectacular. We can easily picture an enemy approaching with guns blazing. It's more difficult to picture a low-intensity battle, a constant barrage of intrusive thoughts that circle round and round inside in the hope of destabilising us in one way or another. This battle is all the more bewildering because often we don't even realise a battle is underway. We're generally under the mistaken impression that the thoughts and feelings stirred up by the enemy are actually our own thoughts.

These tempting thoughts can unfold so subtly that we don't even notice them. Let's take the example of a priest who prays devoutly for half an hour. The experience fills him with joy. Afterwards he goes for a walk. As he makes his way down the street, he notices a young couple walking their children. Some thoughts come into his mind, 'Gosh, I'll never have kids of my own. And I'll never have the joy every dad must feel when a new child is born. More than that, I'll never have a woman to share my life's journey with.' A feeling of sadness begins to fill his heart. The mother and father help their children into a luxurious 4×4 car. Now another thought enters his mind, 'Gosh, I'll never have enough money to give me financial security'. He finds himself picturing the family as they arrive at a large detached house in the suburbs. Now, he feels as though he is missing out on everything. Only ten minutes after emerging joyously from a chapel, he feels condemned to definitive unhappiness.

This concrete example shows that the spiritual journey can easily swing from calm to agitation. If we're trying to lead good lives, God will confirm this good direction, giving us a sense of peace that encourages us on our path. But negative thoughts also come our way, and these thoughts can easily unsettle us. These disturbing suggestions pop up even when we haven't done anything wrong. It's like having a critic inside who finds fault with everything. The fact that these thoughts cause anxiety is already a sign that they are intrusive. In truth, these are the unwelcome thoughts of an intruder; they are not from God. When we live out of a fundamental desire to do what is right, God's presence is always a peaceful presence, never a disturbing one.

Even when we know that negative thoughts are not coming from God, it's all too easy to get sucked in by their negativity. A young monk who was undergoing severe temptations asked a wise hermit for advice. The venerable monk replied, 'When temptations start to speak in your mind, do not answer them but get up and pray, "Lord Jesus Christ, have mercy on me"'. There is deep wisdom in this advice. Don't fight these thoughts in a direct way; in other words, avoid 'hand-to-hand combat'. Don't even consider entering into dialogue or debate with them. Otherwise, before you know it, these temptations will overwhelm you. At the same time, don't just sit there and do nothing; take immediate and decisive action by turning to God. Fix your attention on him, and not on the temptations.

And in the process be honest about your own fragility, by pleading for God's mercy.

As well as turning to God, it helps to turn to someone we trust. The old adage says that a burden shared is a burden halved. The reverse is also true: a burden hidden is a burden doubled. The more we conceal our faults and failings, the more they proliferate. The enemy of our human nature thrives on hiddenness, because it gives him power. He fears openness, because it leads to our salvation. In this context, I remember some words that had a profound impact on my own life. A doctor once said to me, 'Any surface exposed to the light loses its germs'. At the time I was going through a difficult period. I hadn't spoken to anyone about the troubles besetting me. Hearing these words was an 'aha' moment for me. I immediately knew that the dark thoughts festering inside had to be brought fully into the light. The light shone in my darkness, and the darkness could not overpower it.

Father, help me see the truth of what St Francis de Sales once said, 'with the single exception of sin, anxiety is the worst evil that can befall a soul'. Sometimes I'm anxious because I want too much to get out of an unpleasant situation, even something as simple as a traffic jam. Or even when there are no traffic jams, I want too much to get home before dark, and end up driving too fast. At other times, I want too much to get to tomorrow when I'm still living today: when I feel sick, I want so much to be well again that I don't want to allow nature run its course. When I'm feeling anxious, help me to bring my heart back into your presence. I want to regain peace before I try to gain anything else for myself.

Love Delivers Us From Evil

In his bestselling book *Man's Search for Meaning*, Viktor Frankl describes how love delivered him from the evil he experienced in Nazi concentration camps during World War II. His love for his wife kept him going in the midst of awful suffering and deprivation.

A thought transfixed me: for the first time in my life, I saw the truth as it is set into song by so many poets, proclaimed as the final wisdom by so many thinkers. The truth – that love is the ultimate and the highest goal to which a man can aspire. Then I grasped the meaning of the greatest secret that human poetry and human thought and belief have to impart: The salvation of man is through love and in love. I understood how a man who has nothing left in this world still may know bliss, be it only for a brief moment, in the contemplation of his beloved. In a position of utter desolation, when man cannot express himself in positive action, when his only achievement may consist in enduring his sufferings in the right way – an honourable way – in such a position man can, through loving contemplation of the image he carries of his beloved, achieve fulfilment.

The loving thought of his wife gave Frankl the energy to keep going. God is love in the supreme sense of the word, but sometimes even professionally religious people forget how loving God truly is. Instead of turning to God for help, they persist in relying upon themselves. Take the example of Fr Walter Ciszek, a Polish-American Jesuit. Ciszek entered Communist Russia in 1940 to work as an underground priest. He vanished shortly afterwards, and both his family and his fellow Jesuits presumed he was dead. It wasn't until fifteen years later in 1955, when one of his sisters in Pennsylvania received a letter from him, that family and friends finally realised he was still alive. It wasn't until 1963 that Ciszek was set free. He was sent back to the USA in exchange for two Soviet agents.

After smuggling himself into Russia in 1940, Ciszek worked in a lumber camp in the Ural Mountains until he was arrested the following year on suspicion of espionage and thrown into the dreaded Lubyanka prison in Moscow. He spent most of the following five years in solitary confinement. Certain of his innocence, and blessed with great physical strength and discipline, Ciszek was confident he could hold out against any interrogator. But after a year of torture, threats, interrogations, hunger and isolation, not surprisingly he broke down and signed a confession saying that he was a Vatican spy.

Afterwards he wrote, 'I had asked for God's help but had really believed in my ability to avoid evil and to meet every challenge … I had been thanking God all the while that I was not like the rest of men … I had relied almost completely on myself in this most critical test – and I had failed.'

Evil is everything that separates us from God, everything that undermines our commitment to him. We cannot deliver ourselves from evil. But God wants to do so, and in the final petition of the Lord's Prayer, he invites us to unite our desire with his.

Let's finish this section with a grateful prayer by Francis Xavier Nguyen Van Thuan. He was Archbishop of Saigon when the city fell to the North Vietnamese in 1975. He was arrested by the Communist government and imprisoned for thirteen years, nine in solitary confinement. Here is his prayer:

At those moments when I nearly fainted under the weight of evil, you did not abandon me. When I felt tempted to despair and to give up everything, when the storm raged without and within, when the winds of calumny buffeted against my good intentions and actions, Lord, you did not abandon me.

Chapter Ten

For the Kingdom, the Power and the Glory Are Yours

Jesus on the Cross feels the whole weight of the evil,
and with the force of God's love he conquers it,
he defeats it with his resurrection.
Pope Francis

A Hymn of Praise to the Power of Love

For several years I was privileged to live under the same roof in Rome as a truly holy man, Fr Antoni Mruk. This little-known and humble Jesuit priest helped make two of the greatest saints of our era: Pope St John Paul II and St Faustina of the Divine Mercy. On 10 November 1939, shortly before his twenty-fifth birthday, and while still a Jesuit seminarian, Antoni Mruk was arrested in Krakow by the Gestapo and sent to Auschwitz concentration camp, before being transferred to Dachau for the rest of the war.

Although Jews were the main victims of Nazi barbarism, the Poles were not spared. A week before the Germans invaded Poland on 1 September 1939, Hitler gave instructions to 'kill without pity or mercy all men, women and children of Polish descent and language'. Because of this merciless policy, one in every five Poles was killed during World War II, over 6 million Poles altogether. Thousands of priests were deported to concentration camps. Since Antoni Mruk had tailoring skills, he was assigned to repair the uniforms of German soldiers, and this probably saved his life, because he was not forced to work outside in light summer clothing during the bitterly cold winters.

Less than forty miles from Auschwitz concentration camp is the house in Krakow where Sr Faustina Kowalska, the Apostle of the Divine Mercy, died in October 1938 at the age of thirty-three, less than a year before Germany invaded Poland. It is no coincidence that this holy shrine reminding us of God's unlimited mercy is so close to an unholy place that reminds us of our own inhuman brutality. Mercy is how God's love expresses itself when it meets suffering. When we try to build a world without God, it quickly becomes a merciless world. And Jesus, whose mercy is without limits, is the only one who can atone for our horrible sins against each other.

Years later, Fr Mruk became Sr Faustina's postulator, guiding her cause for sainthood. She was canonised on 30 April 2000. Pope John Paul II revealed that this was the happiest day of his entire life. During John Paul's final years, his confessor was Fr Antoni Mruk. They had first met in 1946. I remember Fr Mruk making his way regularly to the Vatican, dressed in his simple black cassock, to absolve the Pope in the name of the God of infinite mercy.

For many years Fr Mruk taught moral theology at the Pontifical Gregorian University in his characteristically merciful way. In our large community of more than seventy Jesuits, he and I were the only ones who liked to drink tea after lunch, so we regularly stood side by side as we did so. Fr Mruk wasn't a man of many words, but even his silence radiated peace. He truly incarnated mercy and kindness. He never said a bad word about anyone, not even about those who imprisoned him for the whole length of the war in two of the most notorious concentration camps ever built: Auschwitz and Dachau. The source of his strength was his love of God and of Our Lady. I can still picture Fr Mruk, in the little spare time he had, walking back and forth on the flat roof of the Gregorian University, his hand clutching his rosary beads, his spirit immersed in prayer.

As postulator of the cause of Sr Faustina Kowalska and confessor of Pope John Paul II, Fr Mruk had a hand in shaping two of the greatest saints of our time. Pope John Paul II's death – appropriately on Divine Mercy Sunday 2005 – shook Fr Mruk deeply, and he steadily declined from then on, eventually dying peacefully in December 2009 at the age of ninety-five.

I share the story of Fr Mruk because his life illustrates the triumph of love over evil. And this triumph of love is at the heart of the final words of the Lord's Prayer. These closing words of the Our Father are technically called a *doxology* – a hymn or saying of praise. They follow naturally upon the last petition of the Lord's Prayer: 'deliver us from evil'. By proclaiming that the kingdom, the power and the glory belong to the Father, we are proclaiming that the victory is his, that he delivers us from evil, and that evil cannot win out over love. This doxology also echoes the initial petitions of the Lord's Prayer, the hallowing or glorification of his name, the coming of his kingdom and the power of his will to save. The kingdom, the power and the glory are his, and cannot be usurped by the evil one.

Jewish prayers habitually culminated in a cry of joy, a spontaneous acclamation. Indeed, it's possible that this exultant end to the Lord's Prayer is based on King David's beautiful prayer of thanksgiving in the First Book of Chronicles, 'Yours, O Lord, are the greatness, the power, the glory, the victory, and the majesty, for all that is in the heavens and on the earth is yours; yours is the kingdom, O Lord, and you are exalted as head above all. Riches and honour come from you, and you rule over all. In your hand are power and might, and it is in your hand to make great and to give strength to all. And now, our God, we give thanks to you and praise your glorious name' (1 Chr 29:11–13).

The early Christians followed a good Jewish custom by adding their own prayer of praise to the end of the Lord's Prayer: 'for the kingdom, the power, and the glory are yours, now and forever'. Although these words do not come from Jesus himself, they witness to his effect upon the early Church. After coming to the end of the Our Father, the first Christians couldn't refrain from giving voice to their unshakeable trust and heartfelt adoration.

Father, yours is the kingdom: may Jesus reign in our hearts and enliven us with his love, forming us into a single royal family, your family, the family of God. Yours is the power: you display your power at its highest pitch when you forgive. Your greatest mercy is given to those who acknowledge their weakness in order to ask for your help. We own up to our brokenness and beg for your mercy. Yours is the glory: may your bright and radiant splendour shine in our lives as it does in the beauty of the universe.

Opening Ourselves to Joy

The words of praise that come at the end of the Lord's Prayer provide us with a snapshot of our future destination and also serve as a signpost to get us there. We proclaim that the *kingdom* belongs to God, as it actually does in paradise, where love reigns. By affirming this heartening truth, we gain extra motivation to do all we can so that God may reign now in our hearts.

In paradise, God's *power* is truly recognised. The saints gather around the throne of God, adoring his majesty, and prostrating themselves before him. In our own lives, the frank avowal of our littleness draws down upon us the power of God. As the Lord said to St Paul, 'power is made perfect in weakness' (2 Cor 12:9).

We are created to give *glory* to God, and we shall the see the fullness of that glory in heaven when we behold the Lord in all his majesty and splendour. This is where we shall find our deepest joy. And in the meantime? As well as enjoying God in heaven, we can enjoy him now. As well as finding joy in the hereafter, we can find it in the present moment.

The jubilant supplement to the Lord's Prayer – 'for the kingdom, the power and the glory are yours now and forever' – is an invitation to joy. Pope Francis has returned again and again to the theme of joy, encouraging Christians to make joy their identity card and the very air they breathe. He is not talking about a forced joy or the empty pursuit of pleasure. He is speaking of a joy that is characterised by peace and serenity, a joy that is a gift of the Holy Spirit.

There is something deeply prophetic about Francis's urging to live the joy of the Gospel. The Trinity is an abyss of joy, which means that joy is not simply good but divine. We are created in joy and for joy, because we are created in the image and likeness of the Trinity, which is absolute joy. But this image and likeness have become wounded and disfigured. That's why we content ourselves with experiences that do not attain the heights of true joy. In his sermon

'The Weight of Glory' from 1941, C. S. Lewis remarked, 'Looking at the Gospels, it seems that our Lord Jesus finds our desires not too strong, but too weak. We are half-hearted creatures, fooling about with drink and sex and ambition when infinite joy is offered us, like an ignorant child who wants to go on making mud pies in a slum because he cannot imagine what is meant by the offer of a holiday at the sea. We are far too easily pleased.'

Not only are we content with poor substitutes for joy; as Christians, we tend to give priority to suffering, as though it were intrinsically more valuable than joy. So much so that Christians are regularly dismissed as moralising enemies of human happiness. As Brian Moore wrote at the start of a short story, 'In the beginning was the word, and the word was no!' There is more than a grain of truth in this criticism. Too many Christians neglect the insistent command of St Paul, 'rejoice in the Lord always. I will say it again: rejoice!' (Phil 4:4). It's worth noting that Paul wrote these words while he was in prison, and facing the possibility of martyrdom! Even though Paul's circumstances gave him little cause for rejoicing, he still had Christ. His joy was deeper than any suffering, because it came from God.

St Paul wasn't just saying that joy was a possibility for the disciples of Jesus; he was urging us to be joyful as an imperative. We're commanded to be joyful, because joy does not come naturally. We must struggle to be joyful: 'no gain without pain'. Yet we're able to obey this command, because joy isn't something arbitrary that is imposed upon us from outside; it wells up instead from the deepest part of our being, where there is a spark, however well-hidden, of the living God, the source of all joy. When someone asked St Deicolus, a sixth-century Irish saint, why he was always smiling, he is supposed to have replied, 'because no one can take God away from me!'

One big reason that Christianity has lost its appeal is because it has lost its joy. Friedrich Nietzsche's words about the Christians of his time were forthright but true, 'They would have to sing better songs to me that I might believe in their Redeemer; his disciples would have to look more redeemed!' Joy radiated from the faces and lives of the first Christians. If the early Christians had faced

149

martyrdom with humourless piety, their deaths wouldn't have elicited much sympathy, much less admiration. But their joyfulness stunned those who watched, and made them wonder what kind of God could give them the power to surrender their lives with such serenity.

Without joy, we are not true Christians. Yet we have managed to transform the uplifting joy that is integral to the Gospel into a stern and forbidding message that drags people down by its grim gravity. We have reduced the dynamism of God's love into a static rulebook. We have frozen the gushing fountain of God's joy, so that it has become ice-cold and immobile in its legalism. No wonder the ordinary person is turned off. We forget that it's a privilege to belong to a religion that commands us to rejoice, that tells us to be happy and that wants our bliss. In this era of history, with so much sadness in evidence, we desperately need joy. We need Christians who are outstanding in their joy, who are true giants of joy.

One way to open ourselves to joy is by mindfully reciting the Lord's Prayer. For centuries, indeed for millennia, spiritual masters have been repeating a similar message: the way to joy is through living the present moment to the full, being grateful to the Father for his loving care, surrendering our agenda so that God can take charge, humbly turning to him for our daily needs, forgiving others, and shunning evil. Deep down we recognise the truth and wisdom of this advice. But we don't put this spiritual counsel into practice. Or if we do, we do so in a half-hearted way, because this enterprise turns out to be more demanding than we expected or because we don't see the instantaneous change we wanted. Our problem isn't a lack of knowledge; the real obstacle is that we fail to apply this knowledge in our daily lives.

As we reach the end of this book, let's begin to put this wisdom into practice by reciting the prayer of Jesus with joy, treasuring every word as we say,

Our Father, who art in heaven, hallowed be thy name.
Thy kingdom come.

Thy will be done on earth, as it is in heaven.
Give us this day our daily bread,
and forgive us our trespasses,
as we forgive those who trespass against us.
And lead us not into temptation, but deliver us from evil.
For the kingdom, the power and the glory are yours, now and for ever.
Amen.